JUST IN TIME!

EASTER SERVICES, SERMONS, AND PRAYERS

Kenneth H. Carter Jr.

Abingdon Press
Nashville

JUST IN TIME!
EASTER SERVICES, SERMONS, AND PRAYERS

This book is printed on acid-free paper.

Library of Congress Cataloging-in-Publication Data

Carter, Kenneth H.
    Easter services, sermons, and prayers / Kenneth H. Carter Jr.
        p. cm. — (Just in time)
    Includes index.
    ISBN 978-0-687-64632-6 (binding: pbk., adhesive perfect : alk. paper)
    1. Easter. I. Title.

BV55.C35 2007
263'.93—dc22

2007006936

07 08 09 10 11 12 13 14 15 16—10 9 8 7 6 5 4 3 2 1
MANUFACTURED IN THE UNITED STATES OF AMERICA

For the Church that bears witness to the Risen Lord

CONTENTS

Contents

INTRODUCTION

In writing this book I have sought to recall memorable Easter services. I remember sitting in a pew, next to my father, one of the few times he attended worship with our family. I remember sitting outside in athletic field bleachers, on an unseasonably cold spring morning in South Georgia, anticipating a sunrise service. I remember leading an Easter service on a date that coincided with the news that I would be assigned to a different church in a few months. I remember the beauty of a deep, solo voice singing "The trumpet shall sound!"

I remember walking to a graveside service on Easter morning in a drizzling rainfall. I remember the Easter Sunday following the death of three wonderful teenage boys in an automobile accident on Good Friday. It is appropriate that I list their names here: Wesley Burton, Andy Burton, and Ryan Shoaf. Their lives, and their deaths on that weekend, have forced me to think about Easter in ways that I had never imagined.

I remember an Easter morning when the alarm did not go off, and our family was almost late for the sunrise service! I recall watching a family leave the campus of the church on Easter morning, because there literally was no room for them. I recall Easter outdoors beside the lake at a new congregation, listening to the wild geese, and eating breakfast after the service had concluded. I think of Easter at Providence United Methodist Church, where I am blessed to serve: the processional, the congregational singing, the reverence for the word, and the "Hallelujah Chorus."

These are a few of my Easter memories. I recall them in order that you might engage in your own recollection: moments that were filled with hope or grief, surprise or order, fullness or emptiness, death or life. In a way, Easter ties all of this together.

- There is grief: "Why do you weep?" Jesus asks.
- There is hope: "Christ is risen," the disciples confess.
- There is surprise: "He is not here."
- There is order: "This was to fulfill the scriptures."
- There is fullness: "Did not our hearts burn within us?"
- There is emptiness: "Do not cling to me."
- There is death: "Why do you seek the living among the dead?"
- And there is life: "I will not leave you comfortless . . . I am coming to you."

I invite you to enter deeply into the truth of Easter. Immerse yourself in the scriptures. Consider the creative possibilities. Put yourself in the place of those who rarely attend worship, except perhaps for this Sunday. Trust in the authority of the story itself. Be aware of those who grieve, but not as those who have no hope (1 Thessalonians 4:13). Remember that resurrection is God's act, God's miraculous act of life in the midst of death. Pray for a resurrection experience this Easter, and for Fifty Days of Resurrection Living, beginning with Easter and culminating on the Day of Pentecost.

Now we begin with a question: Why is Easter so important?

CHAPTER ONE

THE IMPORTANCE AND MEANING OF EASTER

It makes sense to focus on Easter. The resurrection is both the fulfillment of prophecy and the event that transforms disciples into apostles. Easter has historical meaning—the details are given in gospel narratives, each writer offering a version shaped by different nuances. Easter has indirect meaning that is also historical—Peter, who denies that he knows Jesus, later becomes a bold witness to the faith. These historical events take on mystical overtones, even within scripture itself, as in Paul's remembrance of an encounter with the Risen Lord:

> Now I would remind you, brothers and sisters, of the good news that I proclaimed to you, which you in turn received, in which also you stand, through which also you are being saved, if you hold firmly to the message that I proclaimed to you—unless you have come to believe in vain. For I handed on to you as of first importance what I in turn had received: that Christ died for our sins in accordance with the scriptures, and that he was buried, and that he was raised on the third day in accordance with the scriptures, and that he appeared to Cephas, then to the twelve. Then he appeared to more than five hundred brothers and sisters at one time, most of whom are still alive, though some have died. Then he appeared to James, then to all the apostles. Last of all, as to one untimely born, he appeared

also to me. For I am the least of the apostles, unfit to be called an apostle, because I persecuted the church of God. But by the grace of God I am what I am, and his grace toward me has not been in vain. On the contrary, I worked harder than any of them—though it was not I, but the grace of God that is with me. Whether then it was I or they, so we proclaim and so you have come to believe. (1 Corinthians 15:1-11)

Easter is foundational to the Christian faith. Without Easter, there is no Pentecost. Without the Gospel accounts of the resurrection, there would be no continuing narrative of the Acts of the Apostles. Without an empty tomb, there would be no hope of life after death. And without a risen Lord, there would be no great commission. Easter is foundational to the Christian faith. As the apostle Paul wrote, "if the dead are not raised, let us eat and drink, for tomorrow we die" (1 Corinthians 15:32).

Now if Christ is proclaimed as raised from the dead, how can some of you say there is no resurrection of the dead? If there is no resurrection of the dead, then Christ has not been raised; and if Christ has not been raised, then our proclamation has been in vain and your faith has been in vain. We are even found to be misrepresenting God, because we testified of God that he raised Christ—whom he did not raise if it is true that the dead are not raised. For if the dead are not raised, then Christ has not been raised. If Christ has not been raised, your faith is futile and you are still in your sins. Then those also who have died in Christ have perished. If for this life only we have hoped in Christ, we are of all people most to be pitied. (1 Corinthians 15:12-19)

And yet there is more here than historical meaning. The living Christ continues to appear to his disciples, men and women of every age, race, and nationality. In each generation the Easter story is renewed, an empty tomb is discovered, a risen Lord speaks, and a new gathering of apostles is sent forth with a message of transformation and hope.

LIFE AND HOPE

Two of the important themes integral to the Easter narrative are life and hope. The discovery of the empty tomb is a reminder of God's victory over death. The themes of life and death are explored in a variety of ways in this book: in baptismal liturgies, in the Easter vigil, and in the sermons. Luke Timothy Johnson has explored this fundamental question in a very helpful way in his book *Living Jesus: Learning the Heart of the Gospel* (New York: HarperCollins, 1999). A noted interpreter of the New Testament, Johnson offers the following insight:

> It makes a big difference whether we think someone is dead or alive . . .
>
> The most important question concerning Jesus, then, is simply this: Do we think he is dead or alive?
>
> If Jesus is simply dead, there are any number of ways in which we can relate ourselves to his life and his accomplishments. And we might even, if some obscure bit of data should turn up, hope to learn more about him. But we cannot reasonably expect to learn more *from* him.
>
> If he is alive, however, everything changes. It is no longer a matter of our questioning a historical record . . . If Jesus lives, then it must be as life-giver. Jesus is not simply a figure out of the past in that case, but a person in the present . . . What we learn *about* him must therefore include what we continue to learn *from* him. (3, 4)

Christians affirm the refrain of the revival hymn "Because He Lives." And his life transforms our lives, in the present. This gift of life leads to a second profound theme in the Easter story: hope. Had the death of Jesus been the end of the story (as the two journeying on the road to Emmaus suspected; see Luke 24), the Christian story would have been a hopeless one: a good man unjustly persecuted, the good deeds of a healer now concluded, the voice of a master teacher and rabbi now silenced.

And yet the Christian narrative is filled with hope precisely because of Easter. The death of Jesus is real—indeed, he shows his

hands and his side to the disciples after the resurrection. The resurrection is not about the denial of death. It is about God's victory over death: the stone is rolled away; the grave clothes are
cast aside.

Our hope in Christ leads us, quite naturally, to a hope for the
present, for he is the Living One, and his resurrection becomes
our resurrection. We are people of hope. My own experience of
Easter has been shaped by an affirmation written by Kennon
Callahan, legendary consultant to churches and theologian of
God's mission in the world:

> Hope is stronger than memory.
> Salvation is stronger than sin.
> Forgiveness is stronger than bitterness.
> Reconciliation is stronger than hatred.
> The open tomb is stronger than the bloodied cross.
> The Risen Lord is stronger than the dead Jesus.
> We are the Easter people.
> We are the people of hope.
> We are the people of the empty tomb, the Risen Lord,
>   the new life in Christ.
> (Used with special permission of the author, Kennon L.
> Callahan, Ph.D.)

Life and hope are among God's greatest gifts to us. People
gather at Easter, seeking a greater measure of life and hope in
their present experience. Many of them feel as if the door to life
is closed; the voices for justice and righteousness are silenced; the
common good outweighed by violence, corruption, and greed.
And yet they show up for worship at Easter. Perhaps God has
placed a desire within them (within us) for life and hope.

It is a high and holy calling of the preacher to stand before a
gathering of people, announcing the good news of Easter: "He is
not dead. He is risen." Because he is not dead, there is life.
Because he is risen, there is hope.

> Listen, I will tell you a mystery! We will not all die, but we will
> all be changed, in a moment, in the twinkling of an eye, at the

last trumpet. For the trumpet will sound, and the dead will be raised imperishable, and we will be changed. For this perishable body must put on imperishability, and this mortal body must put on immortality. When this perishable body puts on imperishability, and this mortal body puts on immortality, then the saying that is written will be fulfilled: "Death has been swallowed up in victory." "Where, O death, is your victory? Where, O death, is your sting?" The sting of death is sin, and the power of sin is the law. But thanks be to God, who gives us the victory through our Lord Jesus Christ. (1 Corinthians 15:51-57)

NEXT STEPS

The importance and meaning of Easter cannot be overemphasized. You might be a pastor or a worship leader or someone who cares about the faith enough to reflect on this season. In any case, I simply remind you that something important, even essential, is at stake in our celebration of the resurrection. It merits thorough preparation, faithful prayer, and our best creativity. If we are attentive to the Easter celebration, God's story, in and of itself, has its own authority and power to give life.

As you make your way through these pages, my prayer is that these liturgies, sermons, and ideas will incite something within your own imaginations. The book can be read and used a variety of ways:

- The solo pastor can read this book in preparation for Easter. (This can follow a reading of the Just in Time! book *Palm Sunday and Holy Week Services* by Robin Knowles Wallace.) Chapter 2, Prepare to Extend Hospitality, will help you to think through many of the acts of the church in welcoming guests and members into the Easter experience. The chapters on worship services (chapter 3) and liturgies (chapter 4) will prod your thinking about particular ways to celebrate Easter.

5

And the teaching sermons in chapter 5 will guide your preparation in choosing biblical texts for the task of proclamation. Easter worship is one of the moments in the Christian and cultural year when people are most attentive. Chapter 6, The Easter Mission, explores ways to carry the meaning of resurrection beyond Easter morning toward the transformational power of Pentecost. Reading this book once through will help you in the journey toward a meaningful experience of Easter.

• The pastor can read this book with key leaders in the congregation staff, if appropriate; musician(s); and lay leaders in the areas of evangelism, communications, and welcoming ministry.

Imagine a congregation that averages seventy-five persons in worship on a typical Sunday. That church might include a pastor, a choir director, a dedicated member of the church who gives a children's message, another member who passionately wants the church to grow, another long-time member who chairs the ushers, and a young adult couple who have recently joined the church. The pastor might lead this small group in a three-session reflection on the contents of this book. The first could focus on the importance of Easter and ways to extend hospitality. The second could focus on important themes in the teaching sermons. And the third could result in an action plan for shaping worship, evangelism, and hospitality at Easter and in the season that follows.

Imagine another congregation that averages seven hundred fifty in worship. The pastor might gather a similar group: key staff persons, the director of music, the coordinator of children's ministry, the chairs of evangelism and communications, leaders of ministries with young adults and singles. The same three-session outline could be employed.

Each congregation might be led to a very different decision: the church of seventy-five might consider offering a sunrise service near a lake which is adjacent to a park, where dozens of people gather each Sunday. The church of seven hundred fifty might offer an Easter vigil with an emergent feel to it, sending a targeted invitation to young adults in the community. In each case, the common reading and shared planning will have borne fruit.

- Of course, this book can also be read by anyone who cares about worship or the church's witness in a postmodern world. A quick glance at these pages may yield an idea that will make a difference in the planning of worship, in the celebration of the sacraments, or in the preaching of the Word.

Therefore, my beloved, be steadfast, immovable, always excelling in the work of the Lord, because you know that in the Lord your labor is not in vain. (1 Corinthians 15:58)

CHAPTER TWO

PREPARE TO EXTEND HOSPITALITY

Congregations have a couple of options in anticipation of Easter Sunday (or weekend, if you offer the Easter Vigil). The first is to dread the avalanche of strangers who pass through the doors. In this scenario the members are displaced, the ushers are overwhelmed by the chaos, the parking lot is filled, the nursery overflows with the children of these strangers, there are not enough bulletins for everyone, and a sigh can be heard, under a longtime member's breath, "*Next week it will get back to normal.*"

What creates this dynamic? A simple explanation can be offered using the recent work of Thomas Bandy, *Introducing the Uncommon Lectionary* (Nashville: Abingdon, 2006). Easter is a match for seekers, disciples, and traditionalists. For different reasons, persons in each of these groupings are led to be in church on Easter Sunday.

And so we have the first option: we might call this "making the best of a challenging situation." There is, however, an alternative, and I invite you to strongly consider it for reasons I will mention later. In this option, the congregation prepares, months in advance, for those new persons who will come into the church on Easter. You might make these preparations in a variety of ways, but I would suggest a three-month timeline.

Three months prior to Easter, invite the following persons to participate on an "Easter Hospitality Team." Appeal to their desire to offer an inspirational service on Easter to those who come seeking hope and a new beginning. Mention also that you hope, as a group, to think creatively about solutions to perennial problems associated with larger numbers of worshipers on this day. Ask them for help! Remind them that their time will be used wisely, and commit to be in prayer for hope and new beginnings in the congregation's mission.

THE EASTER HOSPITALITY TEAM

<u>Membership:</u> *Pastor, and decision-making representatives (staff or volunteer) from each of the following areas: Music, Evangelism, Nursery, Ushers, Greeters, Children's Ministry, and Communications. Note: This format can be adapted to a congregation that averages seventy-five in worship or seven hundred fifty! Be flexible and creative.*

Task

Three Months Ahead

Pastor—State theme of services and ask for prayer and ideas.

Music—Speak about plans for Easter Sunday, and share any special needs.

Evangelism—Talk about possible ways to extend invitations to the community (personal invitations from members to guests, coworkers, neighbors).

Nursery—Speak about need for more assistance on this day, and brainstorm with team about ways to give support.

Ushers—Speak about the need to be especially attentive to those who appear lost (new to the facility) and about encouraging persons to make space for guests seated near them.

Greeters—Plan for friendly members to be positioned at strategic places on the campus.

Children's Ministry—Share briefly about how the Easter message will be communicated to children.

Communications—Develop plan for announcing the service(s) in the community through advertising, news releases, posters, and e-mail messages.

SHOULD YOU ADD A SERVICE?

Kennon Callahan, in *Twelve Keys to an Effective Church* (New York: HarperCollins, 1983), writes about the experience of a church that is "uncomfortably crowded" (p. 94). If this is your experience, you may wish to add an additional service. Therefore,

- If you worship at 11:00 a.m. (with a choir), you might add a 9:45 a.m. service with a soloist.
- If you worship at 11:00 a.m. and 8:30 a.m., you might add a 9:45 a.m. service with a soloist.
- If you worship at 11:00 a.m., 9:45 a.m., and 8:30 a.m., you might add a 7:00 a.m. sunrise service.

Encourage your longtime members to choose one of the less crowded and newer services, thus making place for guests. In the parable of the Great Judgment, Jesus says, "I was a stranger and you welcomed me" (Matthew 25:35b). In welcoming the stranger, we are not only sharing the message and love of Jesus . . . we are welcoming him into our presence!

The pastor is the essential interpreter and motivator in helping a congregation with its Easter mission to traditionalists, disciples, and seekers. Done well, with advance planning, steady leadership, careful attention to detail, and confidence in the greater purpose, the experience of Easter can be one of spiritual renewal for many within your congregation and beyond it!

EXTEND HOSPITALITY TO ALL WHO WILL ATTEND EASTER SERVICES

As you plan for Easter services, it will be helpful to acknowledge that the congregation will include a variety of persons who are present with different struggles, desires, and questions. While this is true for each congregational gathering, it is especially so at Easter. The following persons will show up this Easter, and while they might not verbally share who they are and where they are coming from, if you have eyes to see and ears to hear, you will quickly discover them.

The Grieving

The Easter message is one of life, death, and life beyond death. For many who will be present in worship this day the Easter message is a challenge. Perhaps a widow is grieving the loss of her husband, or a widower is in church with his two adult children who have come from out of town to spend time together on this day. For the grieving, the experience of life and death is like a fresh wound, and the good news must be announced with confidence, sensitivity, and realism. This may include acknowledging the grief on the first Easter morning (see John 20:13 and the question to Mary Magdalene, "Woman, why are you weeping?"). But the message should also state clearly the good news of faith: "the resurrection of the body and the life everlasting"!

The Unaffiliated

There will be others who have been led by an impulse (perhaps God's prevenient grace?) to be in an Easter service, and they have made their way through your doors. A friendly greeter has smiled at them. A helpful usher takes them to a seat, and treats them like an honored guest. Already, this strange place has begun to feel a little more like home. In the service you will want to preach to the whole people of God, and not just to a sector of it. The

12

good news of Easter is for all people, insiders and outsiders, members and guests. Speak relationally rather than institutionally. Use images and metaphors that are clearly visible in the world (as Jesus did in his parables) rather than experiences from within the temple or the study of texts. Draw the unaffiliated person into the drama of the Risen Christ, and state clearly that this is good news for anyone who will receive it!

The Estranged

Families experience illness, divorce, and relocation. The image of the traditional family—mother, father, and two children—is not always the reality. Churches are often more intentional in their mission to families than to those who do not fit the traditional image. And yet on Easter it seems that everyone shows up—families of four, divorced persons, single moms and dads, teenagers who come along with friends. Whether this is a reality that will continue in the next generation I am not sure, but I often encounter the estranged at Easter.

This may be true for a couple of reasons. First, Easter is a reminder (sometimes a painful one) of family times shared in the past. The estranged want to physically remember a happier time, when that which is now broken was whole. And second, they want to hear the good news of Easter—words of hope, healing, and new beginnings. The estranged may be cynical and scarred but they are present. Share the good news with them!

The Distracted

It is also realistic to acknowledge that some of those gathered will be distracted by many things: the presence of active children, the feel of new clothing, family plans for later in the day, anticipation of a pending family vacation. Don't worry about those who are distracted. Again, they are present. Trust that God will somehow penetrate the distracted thoughts of those who are gathered. A seed may be planted. Allow God to take responsibility for the growth.

The Seeker

Increasingly, persons who know very little about the Christian faith will be present. They are not familiar with the meaning of the garden, the cross, or the empty tomb, and so the sermon will need to provide some explanation. Why did Jesus die? What happened on the first Easter morning? Who were the participants? How did the experience change their lives? Why does it matter to us? The Easter message communicates truth, but it also opens up question upon question. As you move through these and other questions, you will find yourself speaking to seekers, but also many who have spent their entire lives in congregations.

The Home Folks

It is true that you will also be sharing worship with friends who gather faithfully Sunday after Sunday throughout the year. They know the Easter story. They can follow the order of worship in their sleep (no preacher comment here!). They know the ushers and greeters personally by name. The home folks need to hear the gospel in a fresh way, for their own spiritual lives, and they also need to consider how God might be giving them a mission to the grieving, the unaffiliated, the estranged, and the seeker. Greet the home folks as old friends, and encourage them in their welcoming outreach toward others.

The Challenge for the Preacher

The service will need to connect with each of these persons, somehow. As you plan for the day, focus on announcements that are as inclusive as possible; invite persons to read Scripture who represent differing ages and life experiences; vary the music; assume that your listeners will be on different wavelengths. You don't need to tailor the sermon so that it is "all things to all people." Instead, question your own assumptions, and become conscious of the struggles, desires, and questions brought to the service by those who gather to hear your message.

CONGREGATIONAL PREPARATION FOR EASTER

We live in a culture that seems, at times, to possess a short attention span. Many opt for the momentary, and do not appreciate the sacrifices, preparations, and details that make thrilling, memorable, or inspirational experiences possible. This is true in viewing a great work of art, eating a delicious meal, or watching a world-class athlete.

The same is true with Easter. It is possible for an individual or a family to arrive on Easter morning, find a seat at one of the services, open the bulletin, and sing one of the great hymns of the day, perhaps "Christ the Lord Is Risen Today." It is possible for this same person to listen to a message about life, death, and life beyond death and gain something from it. It is possible for this family to leave the worship service with a renewed sense of hope about life's purpose and possibility. Indeed, planners of Easter worship hope for these outcomes.

There is, however, more to Easter than isolated moments of inspiration. Easter is set within a larger context, and this context has everything to do with the life and death of Jesus Christ. Many churches teach this context through the drama and discipline of the liturgical year: Ash Wednesday, the beginning of Lent; the season of Lent; Palm Sunday and the beginning of Holy Week; Maundy (or Holy) Thursday; and Good Friday. Each of these days, weeks, or seasons contributes to an unfolding grasp of the significance of Easter. If we miss all that occurs between Ash Wednesday and Easter Sunday, it is as if we have not appreciated the education of the great artist, the training of the noted chef, the practice regimen of the athlete.

And so, in preparation for Easter, it is helpful to note the significance of days and events that lead to this morning. Ash Wednesday marks the beginning of Lent, and is a day when Christians are reminded of their mortality. If your church offers a service on this day, you might consider marking participants with the sign of the cross on their foreheads, using the ashes from the previous year's Palm Sunday service, and reciting the words based on Genesis 3:19: "remember that you are dust, and to dust you shall return." *The United Methodist Book of Worship* (Nashville: United Methodist Publishing House, 1992) offers a service for this day and guidance and instruction in its use (see p. 319).

Ash Wednesday is the first of forty days (excluding Sundays) that lead to Easter. The forty days are deeply symbolic: In the days of Noah the earth experienced rainfall for forty days and forty nights (Genesis 7); Israel journeyed for forty years in the wilderness (Exodus 16); Elijah fasted for forty days and forty nights (1 Kings 19); and Jesus was led into the desert to struggle with the Evil One for forty days (Matthew 4; Luke 4; Mark 1). Lent is a season of repentance and self-denial, and the days can be marked by a number of practices, some related to the inward journey (prayer, silence, confession, Scripture reading), others to the outward journey (service, identification with the poor, relinquishment of possessions, simplicity of lifestyle).

Palm Sunday (or Palm/Passion Sunday) marks the beginning of Holy Week. The Palm Sunday service itself moves from the joys and hosannas of Jesus' entry into Jerusalem (John 12) to the events of his passion. The most effective services on this Sunday communicate—through words, visuals, and actions—the events of this week in the life of Jesus. It should feel as if the gears of a vehicle are shifting, unmistakably, as the leaders take the participants in worship through the drama that begins in a parade, continues in Gethsemane, and ends in Golgotha. Having experienced worship on Palm Sunday, participants will resonate more deeply with the good news of Easter morning!

Two other days deserve our attention in planning for Easter: Maundy Thursday and Good Friday. Maundy Thursday (or Holy Thursday) is the reenactment of the meal that Jesus shared with his disciples at what is known as the "Last Supper" (John 13). At the conclusion of the meal Jesus washed the feet of his disciples, and gave the new commandment (*mandatum*) to "love one another" (John 13:34). Following his betrayal, arrest, and trial, Jesus is sentenced to death.

On Good Friday, Christians remember the death of Jesus (John 19). Many Christians fast on this day; some congregations offer their sanctuaries for times of silence, or music and meditation; others host *Tenebrae* (darkness) services. This latter experience offers a profound contrast to the light of Easter. For more on Holy Week services, see *The United Methodist Book of Worship*, the General Board of Discipleship of The United Methodist Church website (www.gbod.org), and *Palm Sunday and Holy Week Services* by Robin Knowles Wallace from the Just in Time! series (Abingdon Press, 2006).

PERSONAL PREPARATION FOR EASTER

For years I met on a retreat with a group of pastors (men and women) who reflected on lectionary passages for the months ahead. A substantial amount of our time and energy was given to planning worship (and preparing sermons) for Christmas Eve and Easter Sunday. Most parish ministers realize that these Sundays are the best attended of the year, and they merit intentional and advance planning. In addition, many pastors plan worship alongside musicians, who must make decisions about the Easter service months in advance as well.

The following are three models for preparing for Easter Sunday worship. You are invited to choose the one that fits your context and leadership style, or you may blend elements of these models together. The intention is to motivate the reader to reserve quality time for preparation.

Engagement with Scripture—Personal Model

At least six weeks prior to Easter, take a day apart from the church and from pastoral duties. Find a place where you will not be interrupted—a library, a retreat center, a park, or the cabin or residence of a friend. Turn off your cell phone and pager. Take with you two very different translations or paraphrases of the Bible (I suggest the *New Revised Standard Version* and *The Message*), a hymnal, and a blank notebook.

Begin by reading the resurrection account in each of the four Gospels (Matthew 28; Mark 16; Luke 24; John 20). Read through these passages slowly the first time. Jot down any ideas that emerge for you from the readings. Read each passage again, and after each one write down a phrase or a word that seems especially important. Next, either focus on the lectionary Gospel, if that is your tradition, or choose one of the other Gospel readings for Easter Sunday. Read that passage a third time, in both versions of the Bible. Then, quickly scan the Easter section of the hymnal. In your notebook, record your reflections on the following questions:

1. Where is the good news in this passage?
2. How does this passage connect with some aspect of the human condition?
3. What response is being called forth from this passage?
4. What guiding theme, image, or metaphor is worth exploring in this passage?
5. How might this theme connect with an Easter hymn?

Attempt to write the first page, or the first five minutes, of your Easter sermon. You are not aiming for perfection here; you are simply getting started. Put yourself in the place of the person in the pew. How will you communicate your discovery of good news with them? What obstacles must you overcome? How can you work with the theme, image, or metaphor in an imaginative way? What biblical truth is worth lifting up, and where does this truth appear elsewhere in scripture?

Engagement with Scripture— Small Group Model

At least three months prior to Easter (January would be an excellent time), contact a seminary or college professor with a background in biblical studies. Arrange to take a group of pastors with you to visit with the professor, perhaps over a meal. Agree ahead of time on an honorarium (the cost can be shared by the participants). In conversation with the professor, state the hopes of the participants—a lively discussion related to preaching the resurrection of Jesus on Easter Sunday. Ask him or her ahead of time if any particular resource would be beneficial to read prior to the gathering. As a group, consider a few questions in anticipation of your time together, and ask the professor to prepare to share responses to these as well:

1. What are the intellectual challenges to preaching about the resurrection?
2. What does the resurrection mean in a postmodern context?
3. Can a Christian disciple choose not to believe in the resurrection?
4. What form did skepticism take in the early preaching of the Easter story?
5. Which Gospel account is most compelling for him or her?
6. Can he or she recall a particularly memorable Easter sermon?
7. Is there a theologian or biblical scholar whose work is especially helpful for preachers on this subject?

Plan to spend some time following the lunch conversation reflecting on any new learning. From there, focus on an agreed-upon reading for Easter Sunday (perhaps one of the Gospels). Attempt to connect the conversation with the reading of the text. Brainstorm about possible themes and emphases for the Easter sermon.

Engagement with Scripture—A Staff Model

At least six weeks prior to Easter, invite the church staff to gather in the morning, offsite or in a room within the church where you will not be interrupted. Set aside three hours. Ask the staff to read the lectionary passages for Easter Sunday prior to the gathering. Choose one of the passages and have it read aloud for the group. Ask those present to simply listen. Have the passage read a second time. Ask participants to listen for a particular word or phrase. Read the passage for a third time. After a brief time of silence, ask those present to reflect on how the passage is calling the church to respond. Note these responses on a piece of newsprint.

Once these responses are recorded, ask staff members to reflect on how the themes and calls for response might be presented in the Easter worship services. Some of the possible forms of communication are:

- The sermon
- Congregational singing
- Processional and recessional
- The use of light or fire
- The use of multimedia
- A creative worship bulletin
- Dramatic reading of Scripture
- The use of drama
- Connection with a local or global mission
- Connection with a forthcoming preaching series
- Anthems or other special music
- Participation by children or youth
- Release of butterflies

The difficulty with planning Easter worship (and preparing for the sermon) is that many people think they already know where the story is headed, and it may be difficult to communicate wonder and surprise. The goals in staff planning should be:

1. Faithfulness to the biblical narrative,
2. Creative use of congregational gifts,
3. Attention to the needs of insiders and outsiders, those who know the story well and those who do not, and
4. The connection of worship and mission, exalting the Risen Lord and living as the new creation.

CHAPTER THREE

EASTER SERVICES

For a number of reasons you may wish to offer a number of services on the Easter weekend: people are moving toward the church, in terms of attendance and participation, and correspondingly, the preacher and worship leaders have a rich opportunity to share the fullness of the message of Jesus' death and resurrection.

FOUR DIFFERENT SERVICES

In this chapter, I offer four distinct services. I am not suggesting that you plan to schedule all of them; that decision will be shaped by your local church context, the traditions of worship in your congregation, and the gifts of your leaders. You might consider them, however, as ways to extend the ministry and influence of your congregation at Easter. The four services are: the Easter Vigil (Saturday evening), an Easter Sunrise Service (early Sunday morning), a Traditional Easter Service, and an Alternative Easter Service (non-traditional).

These four different services will reach distinct constituencies. You might decide to deliver a similar message in each of them, and that is acceptable. You are not designing services so that individuals will attend three or four of them! Instead, you are seeking to reach as many people as possible with the Easter message, while at the same time calling forth the varied gifts (music, visuals, reading of Scriptures, greeters, etc.) of your community. If you do offer these four services, pace yourself. If you are the preacher, invite and allow others to lead many of the other elements in the services. Congregants will appreciate the diversity of voices, and you will be able to focus on the one dimension of the service that is your unique responsibility: the proclamation of the Word.

AN EASTER VIGIL

The Easter Vigil is often called the "first service of Easter," and is generally held on Saturday evening after sundown, consistent with the Hebrew concept of the day beginning with evening (see Genesis 1). It is a service that offers profound associations with the Jewish Passover and early Christian practices of baptism. The suffering, death, and resurrection of Jesus were linked to the individual's dying and rising with Christ, and with the journey from slavery to freedom and darkness to light. For more background, see *The United Methodist Book of Worship*, p. 369. More recently, the Easter Vigil has become a prominent experience in the emerging church movement of Christianity in North America that emphasizes the ancient traditions of the faith and the creative expression of them.

The Easter Vigil: An Order of Worship

Gathering

The congregation gathers in darkness, outside the sanctuary or church building, or in the basement. If you gather outside, a fire may be built in the center (this could be a way to involve the scouting ministry of your church). Each person is given a candle as a reminder of the early Christian practice of recognizing baptismal candidates.

Greeting

The worship leader gives an explanation of the service. The
following greeting may be used:
Brothers and sisters, grace to you and peace,
from God our Father, and Jesus Christ, who has been raised
from the dead.
We gather this evening to remember the story that transformed the world,
that Jesus passed from death into life,
and that his resurrection leads us from darkness into light.
The Passover is God's gift of salvation.

Opening Prayer

God of life,
through Jesus Christ
you have bestowed upon the world the light of life.
Sanctify this new fire,
and grant that our hearts and minds may also be kindled
with the holy desire to shine forth with the brightness of
Christ's rising,
that we may attain to the feast of everlasting light;
through Jesus Christ our Lord. Amen.

(From *The Book of Common Prayer*, p. 285, 1979, as published
in *The United Methodist Book of Worship*, 1992, p. 371)

— *Or* —
We praise you, God, for the gift of life.
We praise you, Lord, for the gift of light.
We gather now in the warmth of this fire.
We ask that your brightness would shine upon us.
May the waters wash over us, to cleanse us.
May the bread and cup fill us, to nourish us.
May the word of Christ dwell within us, gladdening our hearts.
May the world that surrounds us know your peace.

(*Silence*)
God of life and light,
give us eyes to see you.
(*Silence*)
God of water and word,
give us hearts to receive you.
(*Silence*)
God of bread and cup,
let us taste your goodness.
(*Silence*)
Amen.

Lighting of the Paschal Candle

Light the paschal candle (from the bonfire, if there is one).
  Jesus said, "I am the light of the world."
  Jesus said, "I am the resurrection and the life."
  (*Lift the candle*)
—Or—
  The light of Christ rises in glory,
    overcoming the darkness of sin and death.
  (*Lift the candle*)
  Christ is our light!

(From *The United Methodist Book of Worship* [The United
Methodist Publishing House, 1992], p. 369; used by permission.)

Light individual candles (if used) from the paschal candle.

Procession into the Church

The pastor leads the gathering into the sanctuary in silence,
processing with the lighted paschal candle (larger white candle).
The sanctuary is dark, filled increasingly by the light brought into
it by participants. Music may be sung or played. Some possibilities are:
  • "Christ Whose Glory Fills the Skies," by Charles
    Wesley

- "Christ Is the World's Light," by Fred Pratt Green
- "Surely the Presence of the Lord," by Lanny Wolfe
- "Sing Hallelujah to the Lord," by Linda Stassen
- Soundtrack: "Passion" from *The Last Temptation of Christ*, by Peter Gabriel

The Scripture Read and Proclaimed

An introduction to the reading of Scripture may be used. One version of this is known as the *Exsultet*, an ancient liturgy that can be found in a number of worship planning resources. For the Scripture readings, choose texts from:

- Genesis 1:1–2:4a; 7:1-5; 8:6-18; 9:8-13; 12; 22:1-18 (creation, covenant, call and testing of Abraham)
- Exodus 14:10-31; 15:1-21 (deliverance at the Red Sea)
- Isaiah 12:2-6; 55:1-11(praise and thanksgiving, invitation to abundant life)
- Ezekiel 36:24-28; 37:1-14 (a new heart and new spirit, new life for dry bones)
- Romans 6:3-11 (dying with Christ in baptism)
- Gospel accounts of the resurrection (choose one)

In essence, this element of the service places the night of the Easter Vigil in the context of Jewish and Christian history. Invite a cross section of readers for this service, as with Advent or Christmas services of Lessons and Carols. Follow each reading with silence, a prayer, and the chorus of a hymn.

Sermon or Meditation (Optional)

The Service of Baptism and/or Baptismal Renewal

The Easter Vigil is an appropriate occasion for baptisms and renewal of baptisms. Use the liturgy of your own tradition, and make the connection between Christ's death and resurrection and the baptism of the individual. See chapter 4 for a Prayer of Thanksgiving over the Water.

The Service of Holy Communion

The service of Holy Communion should emphasize Christ as our Passover Lamb, and the feast of his victory over sin and death. An appropriate hymn for this portion of the service would be "This Is the Feast." You might also adapt the Great Thanksgiving for Easter from chapter 4 of this book.

Sending Forth

After the congregation has sung a hymn ("Christ the Lord Is Risen Today" is appropriate), the people are dismissed with a blessing (see chapter 4 for several examples).

An Easter Sunrise Service

Many congregations have traditionally held a service in the early morning on Easter Sunday. This practice can be traced at an experiential level to the journey of the women to the tomb on the first Easter (see John 20). The service can be adapted in a great many ways. If climate allows, hold the service outside. These services are often conducted near seashores, adjacent to mountain peaks, or near cemeteries. The service can also be held inside (concluding at the cemetery, if your church is in proximity to one). This mirrors the common practice in some areas of the service of death and resurrection for the believer that concludes at the graveside. The sunrise service can be ecumenical, as Christians gather together across denominational lines to celebrate the resurrection. As you reflect on the distinctive aspects of your congregation and community, you might sense an emerging shape for this service. The following is intended to help you get started in this process.

Gathering

Extend a welcome to all, especially guests, family members who have journeyed some distance to share in the service, and to participants from neighboring churches, if appropriate. If the service is part of an extended tradition, this should also be briefly explained, and if instructions are needed, these should be shared (for example, if all participants will walk from the sanctuary to the cemetery). If an offering is to be received for a special purpose (a community ministry perhaps, if the service is ecumenical), this should also be interpreted. It is important that the leadership be warm, welcoming, and inviting.

Prayer

O God, on the first of the week, while it was still dark,
    the women went to the tomb,
    and found it to be empty.
They were compelled
    to share this good news with the disciples.
May we, who have gathered in this holy place,
    discover again the miracle of an empty tomb
    and a risen Lord,
    and may we share this good news
    with one another,
    and with all people.
Through Jesus Christ our Lord; Amen.

Hymn

Be sure everyone has access to the song lyrics.
- "Christ the Lord Is Risen Today," by Charles Wesley
- "Hail the Day That Sees Him Rise," by Charles Wesley
- "Up from the Grave He Arose," by Robert Lowry

The Easter Gospel

Read from one of the following texts:
- Matthew 28:1-10
- Mark 16:1-8
- Luke 24:1-12

Sermon

Offer a sermon that includes the following elements: a retelling of the basic Easter story; some connection with life in the present; a confidence in God's victory over death in Jesus Christ; an acknowledgment of grief and loss; a sending forth of the people to live in hope. See chapter 5 for samples of teaching sermons related to Easter.

Offering

Have baskets prepared ahead of time for this purpose, or special envelopes. Many persons give special offerings on Easter in memory of loved ones, and this can be encouraged ahead of time. As the offering is received, special music can be shared. The following are appropriate as solos:

- "In the Garden," by C. Austin Miles
- "I Know That My Redeemer Liveth," by Jessie B. Pounds
- "Morning Has Broken," by Eleanor Farjeon

Recessional to Graveside

If appropriate, the congregation moves to the cemetery at this time. This can happen as a hymn is sung. You might choose from those above or:

- "Easter People, Raise Your Voices," by William M. James
- "Hymn of Promise," by Natalie Sleeth
- "Thine Be the Glory," by Edmond L. Budry; trans. R. Birch Hoyle

Prayer of Thanksgiving

The women came running to tell us.
Christ is risen. Christ is risen, indeed.
Out of darkness, light has come.
Christ is risen. Christ is risen, indeed.

The tomb is empty, our hearts are full.
Christ is risen. Christ is risen, indeed.
Our mourning has been turned to dancing.
Christ is risen. Christ is risen, indeed.
Our tears have been turned to laughter.
Christ is risen. Christ is risen, indeed.
The stone moved away from the door of the tomb.
Christ is risen. Christ is risen, indeed.
Captives at liberty, prisoners set free.
Christ is risen. Christ is risen, indeed.
Death clothes cast aside to bind up broken hearts.
Christ is risen. Christ is risen, indeed.
The lowly are lifted, the mighty brought down.
Christ is risen. Christ is risen, indeed.
Today the promise of God is fulfilled in our hearing.
Christ is risen. Christ is risen, indeed.

(Michael Williams, *Alive Now*, March/April, 1988 [Nashville: Upper Room Publishing, 1988]; used by permission of the author and the publisher.)

Benediction

Send the people forth with a greeting that communicates confidence, hope, and warmth. See chapter 4 for examples.

The Peace of the Risen Lord

The people will often stay for some time if the service has concluded at the graveside. This can be a solemn and holy experience, as they integrate their own life story with the greater story of Jesus' death and resurrection. If the service is ecumenical, participants will often greet neighbors with whom shared worship is a rarely experienced gift!

A meal can be shared after the conclusion of this service, or a time that includes coffee and fellowship can be offered.

A TRADITIONAL EASTER SERVICE

For many congregations, traditional worship is a great strength. For others, it is not. For those with strong traditional worship, this is the Sunday to call forth your best gifts: varied instrumentation, beautiful flowers and greenery, an attractive worship bulletin, the Scriptures clearly and confidently read, a powerful processional, and if possible a descant above the last verse of "Christ the Lord Is Risen Today." The sermon should be shorter in length than on other Sundays. The preacher should trust that other elements within the service will carry the message as well.

For other congregations, traditional worship is not a strength, but many persons who worship infrequently (Christmas and Easter) long for these traditions. Your service may have the feel of a blended service, but many will appreciate the use of familiar hymns. Again, feel free to adapt these traditions to your own setting. It will help to remember that even in non-traditional cultural contexts, Easter and Christmas services live on in the memories of the unchurched.

Prelude

The music should be joyous and celebrative. Use brass accompaniment, if possible. Have greeters positioned outside the church building, and encourage them to smile as they greet each person entering the sanctuary. Coach ushers to be especially attentive. If the sanctuary is crowded, they will need to be proactive in finding spaces for members and guests. People (especially newcomers) can often feel lost on this busy Sunday. It is best if worshipers are comfortably seated during the prelude, prior to the processional that follows.

Processional of Pastor, Acolyte, and Bible Bearer

The pastor processes to the front and center of the sanctuary; the acolyte carries the light, and the Bible bearer carries the Bible. The acolyte proceeds to the altar and removes the dark drapery from the cross. The Bible bearer gives the Scriptures to the pastor, who reads the Gospel lesson.

Reading of the Gospel Lesson

The pastor invites the congregation to stand. Read clearly and confidently so that the person seated farthest away from the speaker can easily hear it.

Choral Introit

In this and each of the choral selections for this service, encourage the music director to pursue a balance of excellence and joy.

Processional Hymn

The choir processes, following the cross and the light. Readers of Scripture and other clergy may follow the choir. All sing the Charles Wesley hymn "Christ the Lord Is Risen Today."

Welcome

On Easter Sunday this should be very brief, and severe restraint should be observed regarding announcements. It is best on this day to have necessary announcements printed. The focus should be on the spoken welcome to all present. If you will be observing the "Fifty Days of Resurrection Living" outlined in chapter 6, include an invitation to participate in the bulletin.

Choral Call to Confession

The director of music chooses this selection.

Spoken Prayer of Confession

See examples in chapter 4.

Words of Assurance

See examples in chapter 4.

Prayers of Intercession

See examples in chapter 4.

The Lord's Prayer

Print the words in the bulletin. Many Easter Sunday guests will not have memorized these words.

Choral Anthem

The director of music chooses this selection.

The Epistle Lesson

Choose a passage from *The Revised Common Lectionary* or another appropriate text.

Choral Response

The director of music chooses this selection. One option: "I Am the Resurrection and the Life," by John Rutter.

The Sharing of Tithes, Offerings, and Gifts

Many guests present for this service may be unclear about the purpose of the offering. A brief word of explanation and invitation may be helpful:

> The offering today will help our community to inspire those without hope to live abundantly.
> Your offerings support the mission of the Risen Lord in this world.
> Please give generously to God.

The Offertory Anthem

The director of music chooses this selection.

The Congregational Response

- "Alleluia, Alleluia," by Donald Fishel

Hymn of Faith

- "Hymn of Promise," by Natalie Sleeth

Sermon

In terms of length, shorter is better. A fully developed traditional service will communicate the faith in a variety of ways. The focus is quality, not quantity.

Affirmation of Faith

Invite the congregation to read the Apostles' Creed or Nicene Creed. Be sure to provide clear reference to location or provide the printed text. Many visitors will not have these memorized.

Hymn of Joy

- "Thine Be the Glory," by Edmond L. Budry, trans. R. Birch Hoyle
- "Crown Him with Many Crowns," by Matthew Bridges and Godfrey Thring

Benediction

See examples in chapter 4.

Choral or Congregational Response

- "Hallelujah Chorus," by G. F. Handel

A Non-Traditional (Alternative or Contemporary) Easter Service

Many congregations that offer more than one Sunday service strive to incorporate a variety of worship styles: traditional and contemporary, liturgical and alternative. It goes beyond the scope and intention of this book to define or debate terms like contemporary and alternative. This is also not the place to reflect on the wisdom or rationale for providing different worship styles within a single congregation. It is sufficient here to note that many congregations do offer contemporary/alternative services. These are sometimes held in settings apart from the sanctuary (such as a fellowship hall, a gymnasium, or a family life center), and the services may occur off campus (e.g., in a theater or a public school auditorium). I have planned and led services in almost all of these settings, and I can attest that these spaces can be worshipful. Interestingly, while contemporary/alternative services often begin as reform movements against the rigidity of traditional worship, many of these services have themselves settled into a predictable ritual. We are all creatures of habit!

The following order of worship may be adapted to the culture, gifts, and characteristics of your own setting.

Gathering

As the people gather, play instrumental music over loudspeakers. The music should be upbeat and joyous. To supplement the music, you might display the following on a video screen:
- Recurring words of greeting, such as "Christ Is Risen!" "This Is the Day That the Lord Has Made." and "Thank You for Sharing Worship with Us Today."
- Intersperse these with photographs of smiling members of the church and visual images of sunrises, butterflies, and smiling children.

Call to Worship

The worship leader welcomes everyone and invites those gathered to turn to their neighbors with the greeting "Christ Is Risen" and the response "The Lord Is Risen Indeed!"

Opening Music

Adapt the instrumentation for the musicians who lead the service (e.g. trumpet fanfares). Choose any or all of the following, or choose other hymns or choruses that are best for worship on this day.

- "Christ the Lord Is Risen Today," by Charles Wesley
- "Morning Has Broken," by Eleanor Farjeon
- "He Is Lord" (based on Philippians 2:9-11)
- "Jesus, Name Above All Names," by Naida Hearn

Reading of Scripture

- Colossians 3:1-4 (Project text on screen)

Drama

A brief (five-minute) dramatic presentation of a life situation that is related to the human condition to which the Easter message speaks: hopelessness, lack of options, despair, an unhappy outcome, or loss. While these are serious and weighty matters, the drama should treat them in a light, conversational manner, without a need to resolve them. A number of dramatic scripts are available from church publishing houses (such as Abingdon Press) and large congregations (such as Willow Creek Community Church). You might also encourage someone from within your congregation to write the drama; there are often gifted individuals within local churches whose gifts are not called forth. If you choose the latter, offer to review the script and give the writer adequate time to prepare!

Message

The preacher speaks to the gathered congregation. You will want to work with a worship team in preparing slides that illustrate (or communicate visually) the key ideas in your message. Use the following ideas to spark your creativity for images related to Colossians 3:1-4 (also see chapter 5: Teaching Sermons):

- The word "Above"
- A rainbow
- The words "Aim for Heaven"
- A photograph of the skies above

- Visual: a human hand
- Visual: a deformed hand
- Visual: a crucified hand
- The Bible verse: "Because I live, you also will live." (John 14:19b)
- The Bible verse: "Seek the things that are above." (Colossians 3:1b)

Offering of Gifts

Prompt with the following invitation:
>The offering today will help our community to inspire those without hope to live abundantly.
>Your offerings support the mission of the Risen Lord in this world.
>Please give generously to God.

Offertory Music

- "When I Survey the Wondrous Cross," by Isaac Watts (May be performed as a solo, with accompaniment adapted for available instrumentation.)

Congregational Music

- "Crown Him with Many Crowns," by Matthew Bridges and Godfrey Thring

Benediction/Sending Forth

The pastor/worship leader sends the people forth to live with a blessing. See chapter 4 for examples.

CHAPTER FOUR

EASTER LITURGIES

The good news of Easter calls forth our best creativity. Since many who are present will know the basic outline of the story, it is important to discover fresh ways to engage them in the drama of the resurrection. At times this will come through a rehearsal of a familiar scene; at other times the leader will juxtapose the familiar with the unfamiliar. If the leader always speaks from the front of the worship space, for example, this might be a good day to speak from the back, bringing the familiar word from an unexpected place.

As you lead God's people in these acts of worship, it is important that your speech convey confidence, assurance, and gladness. In this way the form of the message is consistent with the content. If your congregation involves lay readers, select your very best readers for this day.

Express liturgical acts with excitement and conviction. *Christ Is Risen!* The good news can hardly be contained! Those who proclaim the good news on this day have the great joy of sharing something profoundly transforming, and as they do so they carry on the tradition of those who were first present at the empty tomb.

PROCESSIONAL

The visual imagery of the processional can be powerful, as the people of God approach the throne of grace. This is a great day to involve participants (especially children and youth) in bringing the cross and the paschal candle into the sanctuary (or other worship space). If you do not ordinarily involve crucifers and acolytes, this is the day to make an exception! The experiential quality of the processional can be very powerful. I have known persons who are not particularly appreciative of music connect visually with a choir processing into and recessing from the sanctuary.

CONGREGATIONAL SINGING

The hymns for this day should be ones known by most of the congregation. In particular, Charles Wesley's great hymn "Christ the Lord Is Risen Today" is especially suited for this particular day of services.

ANNOUNCEMENTS

If your congregation has a formal announcement time, I offer the following suggestions:
- Eliminate the spoken announcements and include relevant information in the worship bulletin.
- Provide announcements on a visual screen prior to worship.
- Limit announcements to words of welcome and perhaps a ministry related to mission, fellowship, or study.
- Include a bulletin insert that lists upcoming events through the summer. This gives the infrequent worshiper a sense of the broader mission of the local congregation: building teams, Vacation Bible School, youth retreat, study series on marriage.
- Avoid announcements that are excessively institutional (reminders of committee meetings or events that involve only a few persons) and overly long. This is a day to focus on the good news of Easter. If you are

tempted to include a number of standard announcements, resist the urge!

THE READING OF SCRIPTURE

Consider reading the selected Gospel account of Easter as your
first act of worship. The pastor can read the passage, or invite a
lay member of the congregation who has exceptional skills in dramatic reading to do so. Some congregations that observe *Tenebrae*
or Good Friday services that conclude in darkness, link those
events and Easter morning together through this reading.

Choosing the Scriptures

If the *Revised Common Lectionary* is employed, the Gospel
readings rotate through the three years of the lectionary cycle.
You will become familiar with these passages as they recur
through the years. The passages are sufficiently different in
emphasis to allow for creative interpretation (for example, Mark's
account is much briefer than that of the other gospel writers).
The Gospel readings, for those following the lectionary, are:

- Year A: John 20:1-18 or Matthew 28:1-10 *2016*
- Year B: John 20:1-18 or Mark 16:1-8
- Year C: John 20:1-18 or Luke 24:1-12

The Epistle lessons are:

- Year A: Colossians 3:1-4 ("if you have been raised with
  Christ, seek the things that are above"; see the sermon
  "Like Him We Rise" in chapter 5)
- Year B: 1 Corinthians 15:1-11 (Paul's description of his
  meeting with the Risen Christ)
- Year C: 1 Corinthians 15:19-26 ("in fact Christ has
  been raised from the dead")

The Revised Common Lectionary also includes a reading from
Acts 10:34-43 and Psalm 118:1-2, 14-24, in each of the three
years of the lectionary cycle.

THE PEOPLE OF GOD, CALLED TO WORSHIP

The "Call to Worship" gives an explicit language for the gathering of the people. Since the Easter psalms are often rich in meaning, you might explore several that communicate praise (Psalm 117 or 150), thanksgiving (Psalm 65, 100, or 126), and wonder (Psalm 2, 50, or 99).

Responsive Calls to Worship

Give thanks to the Lord!
God's steadfast love endures forever!
The Risen Lord is our strength and our might,
And he has become our salvation!
—*Or*—
This is the day that the Lord has made.
Let us rejoice and be glad in it!
The light of Christ has overcome our darkness.
He is risen! Praise the Lord!
—*Or*—
The Lord is risen.
The Lord is risen indeed!
Our weeping through the night has ended.
Morning has broken!
The Lord is risen.
The Lord is risen indeed!
—*Or*—
In Adam, all have died.
But in Christ, all will be made alive!
In the world we will have tribulation,
But in Christ, we have overcome the world!
In death, we endure the long nights of mourning,
**But in Christ, our mourning has been
    turned to dancing!**
On Friday, he breathed his last, and gave up his spirit.
On Easter Sunday, the stone was rolled away.
He is risen!

—*Or*—
Christ the Lord is risen today,
Alleluia! Alleluia!
Christ the Lord is risen today,
Rejoice and be glad!
Christ the Lord is risen today.
Glory be to the Father,
and to the Son and to the Holy Spirit!

PRAYERS OF CONFESSION

Prayers of confession are statements of honesty and repentance before God. We acknowledge our brokenness before God so that we might be made whole (see Psalm 51). We die to sin so that we might be raised to life (see Romans 6). If confession describes our limitations before God, words of assurance remind us of God's power and desire to transcend our limitations, in the victory of life over death. This is an especially significant dimension of worship at Easter.

Prayer of Confession

O God, on this holy morning, we acknowledge the inadequacy of our resurrection faith. Where we have not perceived the breaking forth of your light, forgive us. Where we have been slow to believe the promises of your prophets, have mercy upon us. Where we have viewed one another from a human point of view, grant us the peace of our Risen Lord, Jesus Christ.

O God, you call us toward the light, and yet at times we have preferred darkness. You lead us into freedom, and yet at times we have chosen to be enslaved. Roll away the stone that keeps us from the life that you intend, turn our mourning into dancing, and raise us, with all your people, to newness of life. In the name of the Risen Lord and Savior, Jesus Christ, we pray.

O God, your light rises in glory, and yet our eyes do not see you. Be thou our vision. Your life overcomes death, and yet our hearts do not perceive you. Grant us your peace. Your word is true, your promises are fulfilled, and yet our minds cannot believe such good news. Increase our faith. O God, break through the barriers of our human limitations, and astonish us with the Easter story once more.

Words of Assurance

Hear the good news:
  the light shines in the darkness,
  and the darkness did not overcome it.
In the name of the One who is the light of the world,
  who leaves the darkness of the tomb
  for the light of a new day,
  we are forgiven.

Responsive Prayers of Confession

O God, our plans and priorities
  do not always make space for your interruptions.
Have mercy on us.
We are accustomed to death and disappointment.
We are acquainted with disillusionment
  and devastation.
Have mercy upon us.
We are slow to believe the good news.
We are scarred by false hopes.
Grant us your peace.
We confess our lack of trust, our limited vision,
  our comfort with the predictable.
We believe. Help our unbelief.
Risen Lord, help us to see you,
  move us to worship you,
  send us forth to follow you.
**Let every knee bow,
  and every tongue confess that you are Lord.**
—Or—
Let us confess that we have preferred darkness to light.
Have mercy on us.

Let us confess that we have chosen death
   instead of life.
Have mercy on us.
Let us confess that we have responded
   with retaliation rather than forgiveness.
Have mercy on us.
Let us confess that we are hesitant
   to believe the promises of God,
   trusting instead in our own wisdom.
Have mercy on us.
Let us turn to the Lord and be saved.
Let us gaze upon the cross and see its beauty.
Let us walk into the tomb
   and recognize that it is empty.
Have mercy on us, and grant us your peace.
Let us go into the world, in search of the Risen Jesus,
   and let us follow him.
He is the way, the truth, and the life.

Responsive Assurance of Pardon or Words of Assurance

Hear the good news: the light shines in the darkness
And the darkness did not overcome it!
Death has been swallowed up in victory.
He comes that we may have life, and life abundant.
Christ Is Risen!
The Lord Is Risen Indeed!

Prayers of Intercession

The prayers of intercession link the people of God, the needs of the world, and the activity of God who heals, saves, delivers, challenges, and comforts. Particular care should be given to the writing of this prayer. While intercessory prayer is usually spontaneous in nature it can become a formulaic element in the service.

Aim toward crisp language, delete unnecessary words, and deliver the prayer with confidence and assurance.

Intercessory Prayers

For this day, above all days, O God, we praise you and bless your name. We rejoice in the good news that death has been swallowed up in victory. We thank you for the promised presence of the Risen Christ, among us even now. And even as our eyes are closed, we see the brightness of his rising, and our hearts are filled with gratitude.

Eternal God, hear us as we pray. Your power is great, as are our needs, and these we bring to you:

For nations in the midst of war and famine, and for men, women, and children who exist in perpetual lamentation, and know little cause for rejoicing.

For communities divided over matters of race and violence, education and security, poverty and wealth.

For families estranged, for lost children and broken promises and dashed hopes.

For individuals hungering and thirsting for righteousness, seeking a new beginning, searching for meaning and purpose.

For our own needs, spoken and unspoken, needs that we express to you in silence . . . (*Pause for Silence*)

Our needs are indeed great, but your power overcomes our weakness, your love overcomes our divisions, your light pierces our darkness.

For the strong message of the good news of Easter, which we have received in this place and which we carry with us from this hour, we give you thanks and praise, and as your children we are bold to pray, Our Father . . .

—Or—

O God, we gather in the Easter faith that you have overcome death, that you have changed the very course of history through Jesus the Christ, that you have entered into our lives.

In this faith, O God, we pray that we might be enabled to see beyond the mundane to the miraculous, that we might sense your providence in the ordinary events that shape our world, that we might know that our journeys in this life are woven together with the movement of your spirit.

On this side of the resurrection, O God, remind us again of the message of life and death and life again.

We pray especially for those who are sick and hospitalized:
for those who grieve . . .
for those who are anxious or bitter,
troubled or confused . . .
for those unable to forgive or forget . . .

We pray for ourselves: we too need to be reminded that the stories of our lives are a part of the One great story, the story of Easter, that you call us to be resurrection people, that you raise us into a new life of hope, joy, and peace.

Help us to discover or rediscover this good news.

And let this day mark the beginning of a new life for each of us, not because of our goodness, or intelligence, or intentions, but through your own power and might, which invades the world on this day through the presence of the Risen Savior, Jesus Christ, in whose name we are bold to pray, Our Father . . .

—*Or*—

O God, on this day of resurrection we come to you in faith, as Easter people, our eyes opened to new possibilities of hope, our hearts filled with the experience of new life.

For the renewal of creation, for the redemption in the cross, and for the revival of your spirit's presence, we give you thanks and praise.

We come to you, O God, aware that you have already drawn near to us.

Let the light of this day shine upon us—our doubts and fears, our anxieties and prejudices, our disappointments and angers—and renew us in your image.

Let the hope of this day dawn upon us—our illness and grief, our loneliness and confusion, our fatigue and woundedness.

Let the peace of this day dwell within us—our convictions and beliefs, our dreams and intentions, our desires and joys.

O God of cross and empty tomb, fill us this day with the transforming knowledge that you are with us, to give us light, to give us hope, to give us peace.

Hear our prayers, spoken and unspoken, for we offer them in the name of the One who is raised from the dead, even Jesus Christ our Lord, who taught us to pray, Our Father . . .

THANKSGIVING OVER THE WATER FOR AN EASTER SUNDAY BAPTISM

The Lord be with you.
And also with you.
Let us pray.
Eternal God,
When nothing existed but chaos
   you swept across the dark waters
   and brought forth light.
After the flood you set in the clouds a rainbow.
When you saw your people as slaves in Egypt,
   you led them to freedom through the sea.
Their children you brought through the Jordan
   to the land that you promised.
Sing to the Lord all the earth.
Tell of God's mercy each day.
Christ died for our sins,
   in accordance with the scriptures.
He was buried.
On the third day he was raised from the dead,
   in accordance with the scriptures.
He appeared to the women,
   to the disciples,
   to more than five hundred followers.
He is alive, and he stands among us.
Death no longer has dominion over us.
The Lord has risen. The Lord has risen indeed!

Alleluia! Christ has risen!
Pour out your Holy Spirit,
to bless this gift of water and those who receive it,
to wash away their sin
  and clothe them in righteousness
  throughout their lives,
that dying and being raised with Christ,
  they may share in his final victory.
All praise to you, Eternal Father,
through your Son Jesus Christ,
who with you and the Holy Spirit
lives and reigns forever.
Amen.

GREAT THANKSGIVING FOR HOLY COMMUNION ON EASTER SUNDAY

The Lord be with you
And also with you.
Lift up your hearts.
We lift them up to the Lord.
Let us give thanks to the Lord our God.
It is right to give our thanks and praise.
It is right, and a good and joyful thing
  always and everywhere to give thanks to you,
  Almighty God, creator of heaven and earth.
You formed us in your image
  and breathed into us the breath of life.
When we turned away from you, and our love failed,
  you turned to us, again and again,
  and your love remained steadfast.
You led us from slavery to freedom,
  made a covenant with us,
  and set before us the way that leads to life.
And so with your people on earth,
  and all the company of heaven,

we praise your name and join their unending hymn.
Holy, holy, holy Lord, God of power and might,
heaven and earth are full of your glory.
Hosanna in the highest.
Blessed is he who comes in the name of the Lord.
Hosanna in the highest.
Holy are you and blessed is your Son Jesus Christ.
Your spirit anointed him
    to preach good news to the poor,
    to proclaim recovery of sight to the blind,
    to set at liberty those who are oppressed,
    and to announce the time
    when you would save your people.
He healed the sick, fed the hungry,
    and ate with sinners.
His very presence was and is a sign
    of your victory over death.
He was and is the resurrection and the life.
He led and leads us to freedom from sin and death.
And the meal that we share is a sign
    of your new and everlasting covenant.
On the night in which he gave himself for us
    he took bread,
    gave thanks to you, broke the bread, and said,
"This is my body, which is given for you.
    Do this in remembrance of me."
When the supper was over he took the cup,
    gave thanks to you,
    gave it to his disciples, and said,
"Drink from this, all of you;
    this is the blood of the new covenant,
    poured out for you and for many,
    for the forgiveness of sins.
Do this, as often as you drink it,
    in remembrance of me."
And so, in remembrance of the life,
    death, and resurrection of Jesus Christ,

we offer ourselves in praise and thanksgiving,
claiming the promise that if we have died with him
we shall also be raised with him,
as we proclaim the mystery of faith:
Christ has died.
Christ has risen.
Christ will come again.
Pour out your Holy Spirit on us, gathered here,
and on these gifts of bread and wine.
Make them be for us the body and blood of Christ,
that we may be for the world
the body of the Risen Christ,
redeemed by his blood.
By your Spirit make us one with Christ,
one with each other,
and one in ministry to all the world,
until Christ comes in final victory and
we feast at his heavenly banquet.
Through your Son, Jesus Christ,
with the Holy Spirit in your holy church,
all honor and glory is yours, almighty Father,
now and forever.
Amen.

BENEDICTIONS

It is the first day of the week!
It is the day of new beginnings!
It is the dawn of the new creation!
Go in the peace and strength of the Risen Christ,
And may the blessing of God,
Father, Son, and Holy Spirit,
Rest on you and abide with you,
Now and forever!
—*Or*—

God has exalted the name of Jesus,
And given him the name that is above every name,
So that every knee shall bow and every tongue confess
That Jesus Christ is Lord, to the glory of God the Father!
Go with the assurance of the Easter truth!
Go forth to live in the Easter peace!
Go now to share the Easter message!
Christ is Risen!

Responsive Benediction

I heard a loud voice from the throne, saying,
The dwelling of God is among men and women,
He will be their God,
And they will be his people.
He will wipe away every tear from their eyes
Death will be no more
Mourning and crying and pain will be no more,
For the former things have passed away.
And the One seated upon the throne said,
Behold, I make all things new!

TEACHING SERMONS FOR EASTER

very good possibilities

LIKE HIM WE RISE

Colossians 3:1-4 *us*

If you have been raised with Christ,
seek the things that are above.

That's tough for us. It's against our nature to seek the things that are above. A few weeks ago I was in Nashville, and was able to go to the Bluebird Café, which is sort of the mother church for country music songwriters. Four of them performed their songs that night, just guitars, voices, and about eighty people surrounding them. The music began at 9:00 in the evening and ended around 11:00. Later I reflected on the recurring themes in the songs: missed opportunities . . . taking love for granted . . . the grind and monotony of ordinary work . . . failed relationships . . . more missed opportunities . . . the rapid pace at which children grow up . . . taking the good things in life for granted . . . various kinds of substance abuse . . . broken hearts . . . the passage of time.

By the time we all wandered out into the dark, I had been given a pretty good portrait of human nature. But something was missing: some kind of motivation to "seek the things that are above." I want us to focus on that word, "above." There has to be an *above*. If there is no above, if the dead are not raised, Paul writes, "Eat and drink, for tomorrow we die" (1 Corinthians 15:32). If there is no above, it is just the ordinary grind, the passage of time. It is difficult to "seek the things that are above," but one thing is even more difficult: to make our way through life as if there is *no* above. If there is no above, then this life doesn't all add up. It doesn't compute. The broken hearts, the passage of time, the missed opportunities—"there goes my life," as one of the songwriters expressed it—don't add up. Our feet are planted firmly in this earth, and we are stuck *in*, stuck *to* the things of this world. We live here.

But there is *more to life than this life*. "Seek the things that are above," the Scripture says. C. S. Lewis had a marvelous comment. He said, "Aim at Heaven, and you will get earth thrown in. Aim at earth and you will get neither" (C. S. Lewis, *The Joyful Christian* [New York: Macmillan, 1977], p. 138).

Our feet are planted firmly in this earth, but we *aim for heaven*. We "seek the things that are above." Almost ten years ago my wife Pam and I traveled to Ireland. The Celtic Christians of Ireland in the fifth to tenth centuries had a clear sense of the reality of *above*, the "thinness" of heaven; they believed that heaven started "one foot above your head," and so they built crosses, large stone crosses right in the middle of the fields in which they worked; living reminders to "seek the things that are above."

We are tempted to get bogged down in the things of this world: the missed opportunities, the failed relationships, the rapid pace at which our children grow up. And we are tempted to forget something: We are the Easter people. We are the people of hope. We "seek the things that are above."

I want to ask a question. What difference does it make when we seek the things that are above? Easter does not eliminate our sufferings. Easter people do not deny the reality of death. The crucifixion was real. The tomb was real. And so, at Easter, we profess that *his death becomes our death.*

In Holy Week we understand that Jesus takes our place. *His death becomes our death.* But there is more. If we have been raised with Christ, we live in his power. The stone is rolled away, and we are given the power to do things we could not imagine ourselves doing. His resurrection becomes our resurrection.

You have died, and your life is hidden with Christ in God. The words from Colossians 3 are echoed in Paul's letter to the Romans: If we have been united with him in a death like his, we shall certainly be united with him in a resurrection like his . . . "if we have died with Christ, we believe that we will also live with him" (6:8). And those words echo the word of our Lord himself: "Because I live, you also will live" (John 14:19b).

> *His death becomes our death.*
>
> *His resurrection becomes our resurrection.*

There have been three traditional claims for the truth of Easter. First, there is the empty tomb (see John 20:1-10): Mary Magdalene, then Peter and John, arrive and discover that he is not there; he has risen. Second, there are the appearances of the Risen Lord. These narratives in the Gospels are extended and compelling: Jesus appears to the disciples on the road to Emmaus in Luke 24; he meets first Mary Magdalene and then Thomas in John 20; he has breakfast with Peter in John 21; he sends the Galilean disciples into the world in Matthew 28; and then he appears to more than five hundred people, and finally, in a mystical sense, to Paul (1 Corinthians 15). And third, the trust is claimed in the *transformed lives* of the disciples. Peter, for example, had denied Jesus three times before the resurrection. After he meets the Risen Lord, his life is transformed into one of steadfast love and bold speech.

What difference does it make when we seek the things that are above? *His death becomes our death. His resurrection becomes our resurrection.* And then, *his destiny becomes our destiny.* If we have been raised with Christ, we know that he goes to prepare a place for us. Our destiny is shaped by our decision to walk with Jesus, to live in the resurrection. We are the Easter people. We are the people of hope. And our destiny will be drastically changed as we "seek the things that are above."

Some of you may have been to Disney World. We made that pilgrimage a few times. In his lifetime, Walt Disney received thirty-nine Oscars and four Emmy awards. He created the first animated feature—*Snow White*—and built the first theme park—Disneyland in Southern California. Prior to his death, he purchased 28,000 acres in Orlando, Florida, for what would become Disney World. Due to his untimely death, he did not live to see its completion. At the dedication of the resort, the architect was talking with Walt's widow, Lillian. He said to her, "Wow . . . I wish Walt could have seen this." And she responded, "He did! That's why it's here" (Wayne Cordeiro, *Rising Above* [Ventura, Calif.: Regal, 2004], 135).

Resurrection is not only a memory, it is also a present reality and a future hope. "Seek the things that are above." If Jesus is dead, he is not Lord, and he no longer has a claim upon us. If Jesus has been raised, he is alive, and we claim his promise: "Because I live, you also will live" (John 14:19b). Because Jesus is alive, we want to be a part of what he is doing in the world. Because Jesus is alive, we share in his resurrection. "Made like him, like him we rise," we sing in stanza 4 of Charles Wesley's great hymn. *Like him we rise.* When we "seek the things that are above," *his death becomes our death, his resurrection becomes our resurrection, his destiny becomes our destiny.* To "seek the things that are above" is to say, *we are the Easter people. We are the people of hope.*

"Made like him, like him we rise. / Ours the cross, the grave, the skies." Ours is the *cross.* Ours is the *grave.* This Holy Week, beginning last Sunday, we have been to the cross and the grave. Some of you, in your daily lives, are carrying a heavy *cross.* Some of you, in this season, have been to the *grave.* Today is Easter, and today we mostly affirm that ours are the *skies.* We are the Easter people. We are the people of hope. We "seek the things that are above." "Made like him, like him we rise. / Ours the cross, the grave, the skies."

WHEN AN ENDING IS ACTUALLY A BEGINNING

John 20:1-18

Easter is about endings and beginnings.

Mary Magdalene, on the way to the tomb on the first Easter, thought that she was in the midst of an ending. In many of our communities on this day, families gather around grave plots, placing flowers on them. Easter is about *memory*. The women had gone to the tomb to care for the body of the dead Jesus. It would be a time to remember. It was an ending.

One of my wisest teachers would often make the comment: "What looks like a beginning is actually an ending, and what looks like an ending is actually a beginning." One of our most profound contemporary hymns, "Hymn of Promise" by Natalie Sleeth, expresses it well: "In our end is our beginning" (Carol Stream, Ill.: Hope Publishing, 1986).

Life is about endings and beginnings. Life is a succession of losses. For Jesus it was the same: eating at table with those who would betray and abandon him—*ending*; facing death, a redemptive death but an unjust death—*ending*; feeling the strength and life and breath leave his body at the place of the skull, Golgotha—*ending*.

In our lives there are many Good Fridays. You could probably make a list of the Good Fridays in your own life: days when you have felt forsaken—*ending*; days when strength and life and breath seem to be leaving your body—*ending*; days when you were betrayed and you wrestled with forgiveness—*ending*.

And yet . . . Easter reminds us . . . what looks like an ending is actually a beginning.

Early, while it is still dark, she comes to the tomb. The body is missing. She thinks it has been stolen. She runs to tell Peter and

John. They race back. John goes into the tomb; it is empty. He sees and believes. *It is like a new beginning.*

But Mary is standing outside the tomb. For her, this is an *ending*. That sometimes happens, doesn't it? Two of us can be close together, near the same situation, *one sees a beginning; another sees an ending.* Then she hears a voice, a message:

"Woman, why are you weeping?"

"They've stolen the body," she says, "he is missing." And now we come to the heart of the story. We know something that Mary doesn't know. Have you ever listened to someone, maybe your child, maybe a friend, and they are describing a situation, and to them it seems like an ending, but you know that it is not an ending but a beginning?

We know the story here. She thinks she is talking with the gardener. Isn't it amazing how God comes to us through ordinary people? God's grace never comes to us in the abstract but comes through ordinary people.

She tries to explain that the body has been stolen. He looks at her and says, "Mary," and it is Jesus. And she says, "Teacher." And she goes and announces to the others, "I have seen the Lord." *What looked like an ending is actually a beginning.*

That is our Easter faith.

- Easter faith makes us aware of the One who is with us, even when we mistakenly assume that we are alone.
- Easter faith is built upon the foundation of the One who rolls away the stone, even when we are at the end of our own strengths and efforts.
- Easter faith is rooted in the One who continually teaches us, if we have ears to hear and eyes to see, that endings can be beginnings.
- Easter faith gives birth to resurrection living, doubt as a way to belief, mourning as a way to dancing, despair as a way to hope, death as a way to life.
- Easter faith is about glory and victory, but it is also about fear and uncertainty. Have you ever had the experience when watching a really good movie, and you think it's over—everything has been tied together,

maybe not the way you would have liked, but it is all done—and then there is a surprise?

On Good Friday even Jesus said, "It is finished." And maybe those who were listening were thinking, "*It's all over, let's go home.*"

It looks like an ending.

Maybe you are here today because you're here most Sundays; or maybe you are here because it's Easter. Maybe you are here because you have come to an ending.

Endings are about obstacles that seem too large for us to overcome, like a huge stone covering the entrance to a grave.

What are the obstacles in your life?

- Sometimes *holding onto the past* is an obstacle.
- Sometimes *not seeing the holy in the ordinary* is an obstacle.
- Sometimes *being afraid* is an obstacle.
- Sometimes *doing it all yourself*, in your own strength, is an obstacle.
- Sometimes *avoiding the tomb* is an obstacle.

In life, there are endings. We reach an obstacle, and it seems to be over. But, what looks like an ending, when seen through the lens of Easter faith, is always a beginning. Easter is about *overcoming* obstacles.

Overcoming obstacles is the great theme of the Bible.

Abraham and Sarah are too old . . . *it looks like an ending.* And *God speaks* and says to them, "I am going to give you a child, and from you all the families of the earth shall be blessed" (see Genesis 17). *What looks like an ending is actually a beginning.*

Moses has obeyed God and led the people out of slavery under Pharaoh, and he finds himself at the edge of the waters of the sea . . . *it looks like an ending.* And *God speaks* and says, "Stretch out your hand and divide the seas, and you will pass through the waters" and they make it across the Red Sea to safety (see Exodus 14). *What looks like an ending is actually a beginning.*

Israel has suffered in exile, they have been driven away from their land, their temple destroyed . . . *it looks like an ending.* And *God speaks* and says through the prophet Isaiah:

Comfort, O comfort my people,
  says your God.
Speak tenderly to Jerusalem,
  and cry to her
that she has served her term,
  that her penalty is paid

. . . .

Every valley shall be lifted up,
  and every mountain and hill be made low;
  the uneven ground shall become level,
  and the rough places a plain.
Then the glory of the LORD shall be revealed,
  and all people shall see it together.

  (Isaiah 40:1-2a, 4-5a)

What looks like an ending is actually a beginning.

The writer of Psalm 30 has known illness and danger, fear and insecurity, sin and brokenness. There are times when . . . *it looks like an ending.* And God speaks and says,

Weeping may linger for the night,
  but joy comes with the morning. (5b)

What looks like an ending is actually a beginning.

In the early morning, the darkness is just giving way to daybreak, and Mary is weeping . . . *it looks like an ending.* And someone speaks, and says, "Woman, why are you weeping? Whom are you looking for?" (John 20:15).

And then someone speaks, and says, "Mary."

God says her name. God always says *our* name. And she tells the disciples, "I have seen the Lord" (20:18). *What looks like an ending is actually a beginning.*

In the early morning, the darkness is just giving way to daybreak; the disciples of Jesus know this hour. Maybe you are here because you are at an ending, maybe there is some obstacle in front of you that seems insurmountable, maybe you are weeping . . .

Easter is about endings and beginnings. Easter is about obstacles and the power of God to overcome them.

- Ending or beginning—"In the world you face persecution. But take courage; I have conquered the world!" (John 16:33).
- Ending or beginning—"I am the resurrection and the life. Those who believe in me, even though they die, will live, and everyone who lives and believes in me will never die" (John 11:25-26).
- Ending or beginning—"All authority in heaven and on earth has been given to me . . . I am with you always, to the end of the age" (Matthew 28: 18, 20).

There is a parable about three trees that stood in the forest and prayed about their ultimate destinations.

- Ending or beginning—One tree wanted to be used in a magnificent building. Instead the tree was cut down and used for a trough in a stable, in Bethlehem.
- Ending or beginning—The second tree wanted to be used in the construction of a great merchant ship. Instead, the tree was cut down, and used to build a small fishing boat to sail on the Sea of Galilee.
- Ending or beginning—The third tree wanted to point people to God. This tree wanted to stay in the forest. Instead it was cut down and made into a cross.

Ending or beginning?

Our hopes are in a future that is "unrevealed until its season, / something God alone can see" ("Hymn of Promise," by Natalie Sleeth, 1986).

Something God alone can see. Sometimes, especially at Easter, *what looks like an ending is actually a beginning.*

THE UNLIKELY VICTORY OF GOD

1 Corinthians 15:1-8, 50-58

It is now April. March Madness (at least as it refers to the college basketball tournament) is over. I confess to getting a little bit caught up in March Madness. In my brackets, my chosen teams never seem to make it too far, but what do I know?

What is most gripping for me about March Madness is the conclusion of each game; which game doesn't really matter. There is a loser and a winner, a defeat and a victory. The camera pans for the emotions. The players lie prostrate on the court, if they have fallen short, or they dance in uncontrollable joy, if they have won. These are the extremes of life, all there in living color.

And of course, it is most interesting if some lesser-known school comes along and defeats a major team. We love it when David overcomes Goliath. We call it a "Cinderella story." We are always on the edge of our seats, waiting for an unlikely victory.

Corinth was an unlikely place to find Christianity in bloom at the end of the first century. Paul wrote his letter to a church at Corinth that was less than five years old. He had been their founding pastor and then had moved on. He wrote a letter to them for two reasons: first, there were divisions in the church; second, he would occasionally be asked for advice on financial problems, sexual matters, and family disagreements. Some in the Corinthian community had favorites among the preachers; some thought they were spiritually superior to others; some were trying to blend the worship of One God with other gods.

Paul wrote his first letter to them, and like all good letters he framed it with a beginning and an end. We looked at the beginning, chapter 1, last week—the cross, Christ crucified. The ending, chapter 15, we read this morning—the resurrection of the body. In all of the questions and concerns of life, all of the struggles and challenges we all face, there are these two parameters: the cross and the resurrection, Good Friday and Easter, death and new life.

I love being a pastor, and one of the rhythms of a pastor's life is being in touch with someone wrestling through a terminal illness. The other pastors and I often share this experience, and then the call comes, or sometimes only one of us happens to be there, and there is death. There is a heaviness about death that fills a room—at the hospital, in a home, or at hospice—whether the death was unexpected or anticipated. This is the beginning of a story that happens over two or three days. In facing the reality of death there is acceptance of the cross, brokenness of heart, and weakness and exhaustion. There is confusion. Sometimes there is also identification with the cross: God is there; we recall the death of Jesus on Good Friday. In every life there will be a Good Friday. And there is darkness. And even if we are surrounded with people, it is as if we are alone.

The story begins with a phone call late at night or in the quietness of a room. Then the family gathers, the food appears, and the arrangements are made. The story most often concludes with a group of people gathering, in our cemetery or at another one, and we are reminded of the end of the story. We always read the words of Paul from nearly the end of his first letter to the Corinthians (15:54-55):

"Death has been swallowed up in victory."
"Where, O death, is your victory?
     Where, O death, is your sting?"

In saving this topic for last, Paul is giving the Corinthians and us a clue: in this life we are going to have conflict, we are going to have problems of all kinds, we are going to despair, we are going to die, but we know that the story is not over. Paul wants us to stay tuned for the conclusion that he has been guiding us toward: the unlikely victory of God. "Thanks be to God, who gives us the victory through our Lord Jesus Christ" (15:57).

In the first century, Christians needed to hear this. Jesus of Nazareth had lived among them only a generation earlier. He had died for their sins, he had been buried, he had been raised from the dead, and he had appeared to all kinds of people, several hundred of them. *This actually happened*, Paul said to them; don't give up on this, don't let it get away, and don't forget how the story really ends.

"If there is no resurrection of the dead, then Christ has not been raised; and if Christ has not been raised, then our proclamation has been in vain and your faith has been in vain . . . If

Christ has not been raised, your faith is futile . . . If the dead
are not raised,
> "Let us eat and drink,
> > for tomorrow we die." (15:13-14, 17, 32b)

This is important. Paul is taking all of their problems, all of their
worries, all of their conflicts, and he is saying to them: *"Let me
talk with you about something that is really important!"*

And, of course, the early Christians listened. Their lives were
a testament to the power of the resurrection. Christ had forgiven
their sins. They lived as people who had been given a new beginning, who had passed from darkness to light, from death to life.
The world was changed because they allowed the Risen Lord to
shine through them.

I came across a wonderful image of what it means to experience this new life, to become resurrection people. Imagine that a
pane of glass has been smudged: smudged with sin, smudged with
guilt and shame, smudged with mistakes and failures. When we
are forgiven we allow the pane of glass to be wiped clean, and two
things happen: 1) In all honesty, we become the people God created us to be, and 2) Just as miraculously, we allow the light of
Christ to shine more clearly through us.

That is the good news of Easter: "If anyone is in Christ, there
is a new creation: everything old has passed away; see, everything
has become new!" (2 Corinthians 5:17).

Death has been swallowed up in victory. We are the Easter
people. We are the people of hope. We are the people of the
empty tomb, the Risen Lord, the new life in Christ.

- Maybe you are sitting here this morning, and you are
  present in body, but any kind of spiritual victory seems,
  to you, pretty unlikely. Hear the good news: *Death has
  been swallowed up in victory.*
- Maybe you are here this morning and there is a lot in
  your life that needs to be wiped away before the Son rises
  through you. Hear the good news: *Christ died for our sins.*
- Maybe you are here this morning, and you have felt the
  heavy weight of the cross and now you long for, you

hope against hope for, the freedom of the empty tomb.

Hear the good news: *He is not here! He is risen!*

Christ died for our sins, he was buried, he was raised on the third day, and he appeared to Peter and to the twelve and to more than five hundred, and to James and to the apostles, and then to Paul and, yes, he appears to us.

Wherever there is forgiveness, he appears.

Wherever there is new creation, he appears.

Wherever there is victory over sin and death and the grave, he appears.

Resurrection still happens. Aren't we all waiting for an unlikely victory in this world? Watch. Pay attention. Resurrection still happens.

My friend Will Willimon was dean of the chapel at Duke University and is now a bishop in The United Methodist Church. He tells the story of a young guy, a student who was hanging around after the service—the way people sometimes do, as folks are saying goodbye and commenting about the sermon or the service in some way, and shaking hands. He had not seen the young man before but reached out to shake his hand. The young man said to him, "I would really like to talk with you some day." They made an appointment to have lunch, and a few days later they were talking together in an out-of-the-way place on campus.

The young man said, "I've really done some bad things in my life." Will thought, "*You can't imagine how many times I have heard that one from college students.*"

The young man said, "I really have. I grew up in Michigan; as a teenager I got into drugs, pretty seriously, and it was all down-hill from there. I would do pretty much anything to make the next score. I've stolen from family and friends, and it got so bad that I became a male prostitute. Finally, I was caught using the credit card numbers of my clients, and I was put in prison.

"They put me in a cell with a man who could barely read, who was teaching himself to read by going through the New Testament. There is a lot of empty time in prison, so I would listen to him, I would occasionally help him read, and then in time we would read it together. We came to that story in the New

Testament about the Lost Son and the father who welcomes him home from the far country, and it hit me—this was it, this was true, this was my story. And I knew that I had been dead, and now I was alive, for some reason.

"Well, later I got out of prison, I went back to school, I got into Michigan and then transferred to Duke. And now I'm here. I come to chapel most every week. I just wanted to have lunch with you and tell you this because I figure we've got Easter coming up in a few weeks, and you preachers are always scrounging around for stories. I just wanted to tell you that, this year, I'm your Easter Story. I'm your proof." (This story is adapted from a Bible study led by Bishop Willimon at Pastors' School in Lake Junaluska, North Carolina, July 2002. It is used by permission.)

MORNING HAS BROKEN

Matthew 28:1-10; Psalm 30

On Friday evening of Easter weekend, March 29, 2002, three young boys in our congregation were killed in a car accident: Wesley Burton, Andy Burton, and Ryan Shoaf. These two families are greatly loved by many in the church, and the experience was a powerful undercurrent in everything that was said and left unsaid. This sermon was previously published as "Poking Holes in the Darkness," in Circuit Rider, *January/February, 2003. It is reproduced here by permission.*

> Weeping may linger for the night,
> but joy comes with the morning. (Psalm 30:5b)

I want you to keep that verse in your heart, in your consciousness, for the next few minutes. It has everything to do with how we approach life. It has everything to do with how we celebrate Easter. It has everything to do with how we make it through the next few days. **Weeping may linger for the night, / but joy comes with the morning.**

The women go to the tomb. It is the first day, or the eighth day. It is dawn; the sun is emerging in the sky. It was an act of faith to be there. Some of the disciples had simply headed back home, to Emmaus and other places. They had given up, thrown in the towel.

In the light of this new day, there were surprises: the tomb was not closed but open. They discovered not Jesus but a mysterious messenger. When they did see Jesus, he was not dead. He was alive.

When they meet Jesus, he is still the crucified one. Resurrection is not the denial of crucifixion. Resurrection takes crucifixion and casts it in a new light. On Easter there is great hope for us, but hope and grief are always bound together—you know what I mean. Especially, this weekend, you know what I mean.

Leonard Bernstein wrote his *Mass* in memory of President John F. Kennedy. In *Life of the Beloved* (New York: Crossroad, 1992), Henri Nouwen describes a scene toward the end of the piece:

> The priest, richly dressed in splendid liturgical vestments, is lifted up by his people. He towers high above the adoring crowd, carrying in his hands a glass chalice. Suddenly, the human pyramid collapses, and the priest comes tumbling down. His vestments are ripped off, and his glass chalice falls to the ground and is shattered. As he walks slowly through the debris of his former glory—barefoot, wearing only blue jeans and a T-shirt—children's voices are heard singing, "Laude, laude, laude"—"Praise, praise, praise." Suddenly the priest notices the broken chalice. He looks at it for a long time and then, haltingly, he says, "I never realised that broken glass could shine so brightly." (102)

On Easter, grief and hope are always bound together. **Weeping may linger for the night, / but joy comes with the morning.**

The beauty of the body of Christ, even the risen body of Christ, is in its brokenness. In the morning, when it is Easter, we see—through the eyes of faith—that the broken glass can shine brightly.

I mentioned last Sunday that Holy Week is a struggle. The last chapters of each of the Gospels describe the struggle. They have to do with betrayal and fear. They have to do with disappointment and confusion. They have to do with uncertainty and finally, despair. The struggles we encounter in Holy Week are the same struggles we know in this life's journey. Betrayal. Fear. Disappointment. Confusion. Uncertainty. Despair.

Jesus had been a master teacher, a compassionate healer. But then the latter chapters of the Gospels tell the story of his struggle. It is told in great detail and with utter honesty. When the writer of the thirtieth Psalm described what life with God was like, he captured it perfectly: "weeping may linger for the night."

The good news is that Holy Week journeys through the struggle and ends up in a place that we could never have imagined: an empty tomb, a risen Lord. The good news is that the betrayal and fear, the disappointment and confusion, the uncertainty and despair are not the last word in our own lives. God has a few surprises for us, too! *Weeping may linger for the night, / but joy comes with the morning.*

There is a widely told story, alledgedly about Robert Louis Stevenson, author of *Treasure Island*, who suffered from ill health as a child. One night the nurse found him up, out of bed, his nose pressed against the window. "Come here, child," she said to him, "you'll catch your death of cold." But he wouldn't budge. Instead he sat, mesmerized, watching a lamplighter slowly working his way through the black night, lighting each street light along his route. Pointing to him, Robert said, "See, look there; there's a man poking holes in the darkness" (Peter James Flamming, *Poking Holes in the Darkness: 14 other sermons you just can't sleep through* [Richmond: Monument Avenue Press, 1992], 1).

On this Easter, which feels so much like a Good Friday, we need someone to poke holes in our darkness. And that is resurrection, Easter resurrection, the resurrection of the body, which is at the core of our faith.

One of the reasons we gather on a day like today, an Easter that feels so much like a Good Friday, is that we are the body of Christ, the crucified and risen body of Christ. A good friend of mine experienced the death of his father at an untimely age, of a fatal heart attack. My friend's father had given a lifetime of faithful service to God. When the memorial service took place, my friend could not sing the hymns and he could not say the creeds; his heart must have been full, his mind confused. But he was glad there were other people there that day who could sing the hymns for him, who could express their beliefs for him until the time came when he could claim them as his own again.

I have been in the ministry long enough to know that there are Easter congregations. I love Easter congregations. But I also know that the world has changed since last Easter. The world changed on September 11, 2001. And for many in our congregation the world changed on Friday evening. As you sit here today, each of you can probably recall a day in your own life when the world changed.

There is yet one word to add. The world changed, most importantly, on that first Easter two thousand years ago when God finally and decisively poked a hole in the darkness of our world, when God finally and decisively said to you and to me, and to all who would hear: **Weeping may linger for the night, / but joy comes with the morning.**

It is an Easter that has the feel of a Good Friday. It is a resurrection that has the feel of a crucifixion. And it calls forth a faith that unites grief and hope, sorrow and gladness, tears and laughter. **Weeping may linger for the night, / but joy comes with the morning.**

Our ancestors in the faith named the three days we have been living (in *The Apostles' Creed*).

[He] suffered under Pontius Pilate,

was crucified, dead, and buried [that was Friday];

He descended into hell [that was Saturday].

The third day he rose from the dead [That is today. That is Easter].

He suffered under Pontius Pilate, was crucified, died, and was buried. [This we know. This we have seen.]

He descended into hell. [This we know. This we have seen.]

But let us also confess the faith we believe.

As the first day of the week was dawning, [they] went to see the tomb . . . But the angel said to the women, "Do not be afraid; I know that you are looking for Jesus who was crucified. He is not here; for he has been raised." (Matthew 28:1, 6a)

Let us confess the faith we believe: ***Weeping may linger for the night, / but joy comes with the morning.***

In God's timing—I believe that. And I want you to believe that, too. Amen.

THE EASTER TESTIMONY

1 Corinthians 15:51-58

At every memorial service, someone has observed, at every funeral, there are actually two preachers. There is the pastor, and there is death. Regardless of what is said, two messages are clearly voiced. One might be about hope, the other despair. One might be of celebration, the other of devastation. One might be of victory, the other defeat. One voice might be shouting, the other whispering, but make no mistake: there are *two* preachers.

The apostle Paul knew this, and 1 Corinthians 15 is an extended meditation on the questions raised by these two preachers. Paul knows it is a contested question, this matter of life after death, this issue of the resurrection. And so he draws upon everything within his power to make the appeal: personal experience, eyewitness accounts, logic, history, prophecy, paradox, persuasion, and encouragement. In the end, Paul gives a compelling testimony, one that is the foundation for our gathering on this Easter morning.

Testimony is a word that has fallen into disrepair in our time. And so Christian testimony can sometimes be speaking words that we think others want to hear or mimicking the words that we hear others speak. Christians gather around each other, and we parrot the phrases we've heard, we take comfort in stories that inspire us. This is fine, but it is not testimony.

The word *testimony* is borrowed from the law; and in a court of law, something important is being contested, someone is on trial: corporate executives, a government official, a terrorist, a university athletic team, a foreign dictator. In court a decision has to be made, and in order to make the right decision, the court needs to know "the truth, the whole truth and nothing but the truth." Everything depends on the honesty of the witness. For this reason perjury, or bearing false witness, is a serious crime; without truthful testimony, the law, and a society based on law, cannot exist.

Thomas G. Long, who teaches preaching at Emory, has helped us to recover the importance of testimony:

> Christians understand themselves to be in the biggest court case of all, the trial of the ages. What is being contested is the very nature of reality, and everything is at stake. Was the universe created by a loving and just God, or is the universe a blind and random collection of cold stones and burning embers floating through empty space and unshaped by a creative hand? Are human beings created in the image of God and given lives of purpose and meaning, or is life a "tale told by an idiot, full of sound and fury, signifying nothing"? . . . When we stand at the grave of someone we have loved, can we hope to meet again on another shore and in a brighter light, or is this weak sentimentality and a cowardly denial of the brute facts? Everything is before the jury. (*Testimony: Talking Ourselves into Being Christian* [San Francisco: Jossey-Bass, 2004], 28)

Every one of us is here this morning, as jury, and there are two messages, two preachers. We hear these messages not only on Easter Sunday but also throughout our lives. We are, in fact, wandering around waist deep in messages about who we are, why we are here, and what our ultimate purpose is. Are we defined as people by a photographic image of perfection, or by an imagined bottom line of net worth, or by a respected profession, or by a household of model children? Are we defined as a nation by our level of security? Are we defined as a church by an estimation of success?

You bet we are, if we allow the world to set the agenda. If we don't have a clear sense of identity and mission and destiny in life, someone will come along to tell us who we are. And of course, Easter, resurrection, and eternal life are woven into all of that. It is fundamental. Do I think that this life is all there is? That's death preaching to me. Paul heard the voice of that preacher, he had wrestled with the implications of that logic, and he knew where it ended. If this life is all there is, he said, then our preaching is in vain, and your faith is in vain. If this life is all there is then eat and drink, for tomorrow we die (see 1 Corinthians 15:32).

That is the message that comes across to us in a culture of death: Eat, drink, and be merry, for tomorrow you die. Do you remember the bumper sticker: The one who dies with the most toys wins? It is an honest, secular vision of life. I respect it, even if I do not agree with it, even if I believe that it is false witness.

There is more. There has to be more. And that is why we're here. Something is at stake at Easter. If you live long enough, you see people suffer. If you live long enough, you catch yourself waiting for test results. If you live long enough, you see people you love die. If you live long enough, you find yourself standing at gravesides.

And that is where Easter comes in. Easter is all about the death of Jesus. But Easter is more. The good news is that God has raised Jesus from the dead. And the even better news is that God will raise us from the dead and give us a new life, an eternal life.

That's good news.

Paul knew something was at stake, and he had to tell this news truthfully. What was the alternative? "If Christ has not been raised, then our proclamation has been in vain and your faith has been in vain" (1 Corinthians 15:14). In other words, if Easter is not true, I might as well be out hitting a tennis ball; you might as well be leaning over a golf club or turning over from the last nap.

It the dead are not raised, Paul said, let us eat and drink, for tomorrow we die.

And so the Easter message comes as an insistence on truth. "Death has been swallowed up in victory" (1 Corinthians 15:54b).

"Swallowed up in victory"

Easter is all about the victory of God. Again, there is a need for clarity. This is why, in sports, the umpiring matters, the refereeing matters, and the scoreboard matters. We want to know who has prevailed. For a time, we cannot be certain. But in the end, there is a victory, for someone.

The Christian wonders, is it death or life? Is it all meaningless, or is there a purpose? Are we cursed or blessed? Is it about the love of power or the power of love?

What is it?

Cassie Bernall, who was a promising student, walked into Columbine High School on a Tuesday morning. Soon the high school became a war zone. Cassie's story is told by her mother, Misty Bernall, in *She Said Yes* (Harrisburg: Plough, 1999).

"Do you believe in God?" one of the heavily armed gunmen asked the blonde girl reading her Bible in the library while the school was under siege.

"Yes, I believe in God," she replied in a voice that was strong enough to be heard by classmates hidden beneath the nearby tables and desks.

The gunman in the long black trench coat laughed, "Why?" he asked mockingly. Then he raised his gun and shot and killed seventeen-year-old Cassie Bernall.

It seems that Cassie must have had a premonition. She had reflected on these questions of life and death. When it became apparent that she was not coming home that terrible Tuesday, her brother found her notebook lying on a desk, filled with words that echoed the testimony of the apostle Paul:

> More than that, I regard everything as loss because of the surpassing value of knowing Christ Jesus my Lord. For his sake I have suffered the loss of all things, and I regard them as rubbish, in order that I may gain Christ and be found in him, not having a righteousness of my own that comes from the law, but one that comes through faith in Christ, the righteousness from God based on faith. I want to know Christ and the power of his resurrection and the sharing of his sufferings by becoming like

him in his death, if somehow I may attain the resurrection from the dead. (Philippians 3:8-11)

For a time it is contested. But in the end, death is "swallowed up in victory." In the spiritual classic *Pilgrim's Progress*, John Bunyan has Christian walking along the road, when to his horror he notices ferocious lions standing in his path. There is no way he can avoid the animals or the situation. He is terrified, but he continues to walk. Then, he is delighted to learn that the lions are chained to a post. Someone has made this journey before him and has tamed the lions. Although Christian has to make this journey, someone has made the road safe for him. Someone has disarmed the hostile creatures. The lions remain, but the threat has been removed.

"Death has been swallowed up in victory. Where, O death, is your victory? Where, O death, is your sting?" (1 Corinthians 15:54b-55).

This is not the denial of death. The women go to the tomb, the gospel writers tell us, "while it is still dark" (John 20:1). We are not pretending that death is not real, that it holds no power.

We *are* affirming that *death has been swallowed up in victory*. This is a statement of faith, of affirmation of hope. The resurrection sets before us a decision. In the words of character Andy Defreyne in the movie *The Shawshank Redemption*, "You either get busy living or get busy dying." In the dilemma facing Christian in *Pilgrim's Progress*, *you either keep walking or you turn back*. In the grief of those women who woke up early and went to the tomb, while it was still dark, *you either give up or you turn to the Lord*. In the meditation of Cassie Bernall, it is to *give up everything else and suffer, die, and rise with Christ*.

On Easter, in life, there are two preachers, there are two voices, there are two paths. The first sentence in the *Didache*—the earliest known Christian document outside of the New Testament canon—reads: "There are two ways, one of life and one of death, and there is a great difference between the two ways."

The good news, brothers and sisters, is that this is true. Christ is risen. The Lord is risen indeed. Death has been swallowed up in victory, and how can we respond? With the words of the apostle Paul: "Thanks be to God, who gives us the victory through our Lord Jesus Christ" (1 Corinthians 15:57).

Who gives *us* the victory . . . "Therefore," Paul adds, "be steadfast, immovable, always excelling in the work of the Lord, because you know that in the Lord your labor is not in vain" (v. 58). And so let us go forth to live as resurrected people.

Love's redeeming work is done, Alleluia!
Fought the fight, the battle won, Alleluia!
Death in vain forbids him rise, Alleluia!
Christ has opened paradise, Alleluia!

("Christ the Lord Is Risen Today," by Charles Wesley, stanza 2)

CHAPTER SIX

EASTER MISSION: NOT AN ENDING BUT A BEGINNING

The pastor or worship leader is tempted to experience the Easter celebration as an ending of sorts. In many congregations there is a movement and a momentum from Advent to Christmas, and then, after the beginning of the calendar year and the organization of the community's leadership and finances, there is the journey from Lent to Easter. After Easter Sunday, it is natural for those who have envisioned and implemented the experiences to be physically and emotionally exhausted.

As natural as this reality seems to our energy level or programmatic vision, I want to suggest an alternative, one that is consistent with Scripture, the motivations of those who worship, and the needs of those who surround us in the culture. This alternative can be expressed in a simple sentence: *Easter is a beginning, not an ending.* The Gospel accounts of Jesus' post-resurrection appearances provide evidence and inspiration for this view.

THE EASTER MISSION IN THE GOSPEL ACCOUNTS

Matthew

As Matthew tells the story, the women go to the tomb at daybreak on Sunday. A messenger speaks to them and after announcing the resurrection of Jesus, sends them to Galilee: "There you will see him" (28:7c). On the way they encounter Jesus himself, who again commands them to leave for Galilee, and to invite the brothers. As they reach Galilee, Jesus is present on a mountain. In that place they worship him, and he gives them the great commission:

> Now the eleven disciples went to Galilee, to the mountain to which Jesus had directed them. When they saw him, they worshiped him; but some doubted. And Jesus came and said to them, "All authority in heaven and on earth has been given to me. Go therefore and make disciples of all nations, baptizing them in the name of the Father and of the Son and of the Holy Spirit, and teaching them to obey everything that I have commanded you. And remember, I am with you always, to the end of the age." (Matthew 28:16-20)

What seemed like an ending—the death of Jesus—is now, through the power of the resurrection, a commission to make disciples of all nations . . . a new beginning.

Luke

In Luke's Gospel, the women come to the tomb on Sunday morning to anoint the body of Jesus with spices. When they arrive the stone has been rolled away and the body is missing. They are afraid when two men in dazzling clothes appear and ask them a question: "Why do you look for the living among the dead?" (24:5b). The women then tell the story of their encounter to the apostles, who do not believe them. Luke's narrative then shifts to the experience of two of the disciples with Jesus on the

76

road to Emmaus. They are unaware that he is present with them until he breaks bread with them, and then "their eyes were opened" (24:31).

These disciples return to Jerusalem, and there they meet with the others and share their witness of an encounter with the Risen Lord. While the group is gathered, Jesus appears to them; he invites them to touch him, and they eat a meal together. He then gives them instructions about the future:

> Then he said to them, "These are my words that I spoke to you while I was still with you—that everything written about me in the law of Moses, the prophets, and the psalms must be fulfilled." Then he opened their minds to understand the scriptures, and he said to them, "Thus it is written, that the Messiah is to suffer and to rise from the dead on the third day, and that repentance and forgiveness of sins is to be proclaimed in his name to all nations, beginning from Jerusalem. You are witnesses of these things. And see, I am sending upon you what my Father promised; so stay here in the city until you have been clothed with power from on high." (Luke 24:44-49)

Then Jesus blesses them. Luke's story, of course, continues in the book of Acts, with the promise that the disciples will receive power when the Holy Spirit comes upon then, the command that they will be Jesus' "witnesses in Jerusalem, in all Judea and Samaria, and to the ends of the earth." This promise is immediately followed by the ascension of Jesus (Acts 1:6-11).

What seemed like an ending—the death of Jesus—is now, through the power of the resurrection, an experience of the Holy Spirit and a command to be witnesses to the Living Christ . . . a new beginning.

John

In John's Gospel, Mary Magdalene comes to the tomb on Easter morning while it is still dark. She sees that the stone has been rolled away, and she runs to Peter and the disciple whom Jesus loved (perhaps John?). On the basis of the empty tomb,

John believes. As Mary stands weeping outside the tomb, two messengers greet her with a question: "Woman, why are you weeping?" (20:13). She turns and sees someone she imagines is the gardener, but then, when her name is spoken, she realizes that it is the Risen Lord. He commands her to tell his brothers that he is ascending to be with the Father.

That evening Jesus breathes on the disciples and gives them the Holy Spirit; a week later he allows Thomas to touch his wounds. In a later appearance, he greets Peter and some of the other disciples after a night of fishing. After they have breakfast together, Jesus asks Peter the same question three times: "Do you love me?" He correspondingly gives Peter three commandments: "Feed my lambs," "Tend my sheep," "Feed my sheep." Then Jesus says to Peter, "Follow me" (see 21:1-23). Interestingly, the last two chapters of John conclude with open-ended summary statements:

> Now Jesus did many other signs in the presence of his disciples, which are not written in this book. But these are written so that you may come to believe that Jesus is the Messiah, the Son of God, and that through believing you may have life in his name. (John 20:30-31)

> But there are also many other things that Jesus did; if every one of them were written down, I suppose that the world itself could not contain the books that would be written. (John 21:25)

What seemed like an ending—the death of Jesus—has become, through the presence of the Living Christ, a call to feed God's sheep and to follow Jesus . . . a new beginning.

You will want to connect those who are present on Easter with the same commissions that the Risen Christ gave to his first followers, a call to carry out his purposes for the church and the world. These callings are, very simply, to make disciples (Matthew), to receive the power of the Holy Spirit as witnesses (Luke), and to feed his sheep (John).

Easter is not a spectacle to be observed, like the climax in a symphony of beautiful orchestral music. Easter is not an ending. Easter is a beginning.

THE EASTER MISSION IN THE *Used 2017* CONGREGATION: FIFTY DAYS OF *printed* RESURRECTION LIVING *a devotional from the following*

Many congregations are accustomed to forty-day programs of spiritual growth (such as Rick Warren's *Purpose-Driven Life*, from the experience of Saddleback Community Church in California, or Lenten calls to self-denial and spiritual renewal). The season of Easter is often referred to as "The Great Fifty Days" (also known as "Eastertide), including the seven Sundays prior to Pentecost (see Acts 2). The Ascension is observed as the fortieth day and Pentecost as the fiftieth day. The fifty days can be a time of reflection on the resurrection of Jesus, the kingdom of God, prayer for God's presence and power, and anticipation of the coming of the Holy Spirit.

The following is a simple format for individuals or small groups to use in linking the resurrection of Jesus with the mission that he gave to the disciples after the resurrection. The lectionary is followed to some extent, but this can be modified according to the culture of your congregation. Each day includes a verse of Scripture, a guide to action, and a prayer.

Day One (Easter Sunday)

Worship with your congregation, and join with them in the reading of Scripture and prayers. As you depart, ask how God is calling you to respond to the Easter message.

Day Two

Scripture: Matthew 28:6a. "He is not here; for he has been raised."

Action: Pray for Christian congregations throughout the world that are witnesses to the message of Easter.

Prayer: *We thank you, God, for the miracle of Easter.*

Day Three

Scripture: Matthew 28:7b. "He is going ahead of you to Galilee."

Action: Follow Jesus wherever he leads.

Prayer: *Help me follow Jesus, so that I might hear his teachings.*

Day Four

Scripture: Matthew 28:8. "They left the tomb quickly with fear and great joy, and ran to tell his disciples."

Action: Gladly bear witness to your faith.

Prayer: *Let me see evangelism not as a duty, O Lord, but as a delight.*

Day Five

Scripture: Mark 16:6. "Do not be alarmed . . . Jesus of Nazareth, who was crucified . . . has been raised."

Action: Seek to know the calmness and peace of God in the face of death.

Prayer: *Let me trust you, O God, in life and in death.*

Day Six

Scripture: Mark 16:4. "The stone, which was very large, had already been rolled back."

Action: Live in the strength and power of God, and not only in your own resources.

Prayer: *Where I am weak, O Lord, you are strong.*

Day Seven

A day of rest. Reflect on the freedom that is ours in the Risen Christ.

Day Eight

Worship with your congregation, and join with them in the reading of Scripture and prayers. As you depart, ask how you are being called to action.

Day Nine

Scripture: Luke 24:5b. "Why do you look for the living among the dead?"

Action: Support ministries that occur in situations that seem hopeless: prisons and hospices.

Prayer: *I praise you, O God, for you are the resurrection and the life.*

Day Ten

Scripture: Luke 24:35a. "Then they told what had happened on the road."

Action: Share a meal with a trusted Christian friend and share your experience of Jesus.

Prayer: *Thank you, Jesus, for walking alongside us in this life's journey.*

Day Eleven

Scripture: Luke 24:29b. "Stay with us."

Action: Make a place in your life, in your home, in your schedule, for Jesus.

Prayer: *Help me welcome you, Jesus. Enter into my life.*

Day Twelve

Scripture: Luke 24:30b. "He took bread, blessed and broke it, and gave it to them."

Action: Receive the eucharist as a symbol of God's grace.

Prayer: *Sustain us with manna from heaven. Give us this day our daily bread.*

Day Thirteen

Scripture: Luke 24:39b. "Touch me and see; for a ghost does not have flesh and bones."

Action: Touch the body of Christ, in the poor, the hungry, the imprisoned, the stranger.

Prayer: *Help me to see you today, Lord Jesus; help me know that you are real.*

Day Fourteen

A day of rest. Reflect on the gift of eternal life. Listen to Handel's *Messiah.*

Day Fifteen

Worship with your congregation, and join with them in the reading of Scripture and prayers. As you depart, ask how you are being called to action.

Day Sixteen

Scripture: John 20:19b. "Jesus came and stood among them and said, 'Peace be with you.'"

Action: Offer the peace of Christ, in concrete ways, to others.

Prayer: *Risen Lord Jesus, make me an instrument of your peace.*

Day Seventeen

Scripture: John 20:22. "He breathed on them and said to them, 'Receive the Holy Spirit.'"

Action: Take deep breaths, inhaling and exhaling.
Remember that God's Spirit/Breath sustains
you.

Prayer: *Fill me with your Spirit, O God.*

Day Eighteen

Scripture: John 20:21b. "As the Father has sent me, so I
send you."

Action: Imagine that Jesus is sending you into a particular situation today. Where might that be?

Prayer: *I thank you, Lord Jesus, for the promise that you
are always with me.*

Day Nineteen

Scripture: John 20:27. "[Jesus] said to Thomas, '. . . Reach
out your hand and put it in my side.'"

Action: Consider how the body of Christ is wounded in
our world. How can you be an agent of recon-
ciliation and peace?

Prayer: *I pray for a broken world, O God, that all people
might be made whole.*

Day Twenty

Scripture: John 20:29b. "Blessed are those who have not
seen and yet have come to believe."

Action: Take a step in faith and trust today, a step that
involves some risk.

Prayer: *I cannot always see you, God, but I know that you
are present.*

Day Twenty-one

A day of rest. Remember that eternal life is a gift. Reflect on
the gifts that enrich your life.

Day Twenty-two

Worship with your congregation, and join with them in the reading of Scripture and prayers. As you depart, ask how you are being called to action.

Day Twenty-three

Scripture: Matthew 28:18. "Jesus came and said to them, 'All authority in heaven and on earth has been given to me.'"

Action: Live under the authority of Jesus. Offer this day to him.

Prayer: *Not my will, O Lord, but your will be done.*

Day Twenty-four

Scripture: Matthew 28:19a. Jesus said, "Go . . . and make disciples."

Action: Find a concrete way to support those who teach Sunday school in your congregation.

Prayer: *Teach me your ways, O Lord. Show me your paths.*

Day Twenty-five

Scripture: Matthew 28:19b. "Make disciples of all nations."

Action: Find a way to learn more about disciple making in another part of the world.

Prayer: *Offer a prayer of intercession for brothers and sisters in Christ in Asia, Africa, or Latin America.*

Day Twenty-six

Scripture: Matthew 28:19c. " . . . baptizing them in the name of the Father and of the Son and of the Holy Spirit."

Action: Remember your baptism, and be thankful!

Prayer: *Cleanse me of my sin, O God. Renew a right spirit within me.*

Day Twenty-seven

Scripture: Matthew 28:20a. " . . . teaching them to obey everything that I have commanded you."
Action: Listen to the teachings of Jesus, especially in the Sermon on the Mount (Matthew 5–7). Which teaching seems most difficult?
Prayer: *If I neglect your laws, O God, have mercy on me.*

Day Twenty-eight

A day of rest. Spend time in silence and solitude. Open your heart and mind to the peace of the Risen Christ.

Day Twenty-nine

Worship with your congregation, and join with them in the reading of Scripture and prayers. As you depart, ask how you are being called to action.

Day Thirty

Scripture: Matthew 28:20b. "I am with you always."
Action: Live in the assurance that Jesus walks beside you today.
Prayer: *Keep before me the truth, O Lord, that I am never alone.*

Day Thirty-one

Scripture: Luke 24:44b. "Everything written about me in the law of Moses, the prophets, and the psalms must be fulfilled."
Action: Trust in the authority of Scripture.
Prayer: *Let me believe the truths found in your Word, O God.*

Day Thirty-two

Scripture: Luke 24:45. "Then he opened their minds to understand the scriptures."

Action: Study the endings of each of the four Gospels (Matthew 28; Mark 16; Luke 24; John 20–21).

Prayer: *Open my mind and heart, O Lord. Let me be receptive to truths I do not now know.*

Day Thirty-three

Scripture: Luke 24:46b-47a. "The Messiah is to suffer and to rise from the dead on the third day, and . . . repentance and forgiveness of sins is to be proclaimed in his name."

Action: Confess the sins that separate you from those you have offended.

Prayer: *Help me resist evil, O God, and embrace that which is pleasing in your sight.*

Day Thirty-four

Scripture: Luke 24:49b. "Stay here in the city until you have been clothed with power from on high."

Action: If you are not sure about the next step in your life, wait, and give time to prayer and discernment.

Prayer: *Your ways are not my ways, O God. Your plans are not my plans. Give me patience.*

Day Thirty-five

A day of rest. The Risen Christ gently greets you with a command: "Do not be afraid" (Matthew 28:10). Let go of your fears, and trust in this promise.

Day Thirty-six

Worship with your congregation, and join with them in the reading of Scripture and prayers. As you depart, ask how you are being called to action.

Day Thirty-seven

Scripture: John 21:12. "Jesus said to them, 'Come and have breakfast.'"

   Action: Support a hunger ministry that serves people in the name of Jesus.

   Prayer: *For those who hunger, give bread. For those who have bread, give a hunger for justice and righteousness.*

Day Thirty-eight

Scripture: John 21:15b. "Jesus said to Simon Peter, ' . . . do you love me . . .?'"

   Action: Take care of a need in your community, because of your love for Jesus.

   Prayer: *Increase my love for you, O God, and expand my love for my neighbor.*

Day Thirty-nine

Scripture: John 21:16c. "Jesus said to him, 'Tend my sheep.'"

   Action: Who are the lost in your community? Can you find them and help them?

   Prayer: *Give me compassion, O God, for those who are lost and alone.*

Day Forty—Day of Ascension

Scripture: Acts 1:9b. "As they were watching, he was lifted up."

   Action: Trust that the ultimate power of the universe belongs to God.

   Prayer: *Help me not to be discouraged, O God, when the world seems to be in a perpetual state of crisis.*

Day Forty-one

Scripture: Acts 1:6b. "Lord, is this the time when you will restore the kingdom . . .?"

Action: Live faithfully each day without knowing the specifics of God's long-range plans.

Prayer: *This is the day that you have made, O God. Let me be glad and rejoice in it.*

Day Forty-two

A day of rest. Remember that Jesus is the Alpha and the Omega, the beginning and the end, the first and the last (see Revelation 22:13). Trust the future to God.

Day Forty-three

Worship with your congregation, and join with them in the reading of Scripture and prayers. As you depart, ask how you are being called to action.

Day Forty-four

Scripture: Acts 1:8. "You will be my witnesses . . ."

Action: Share your faith experience truthfully and humbly with someone today.

Prayer: *Give me the confidence that you are speaking through me, O Lord, when I speak about you.*

Day Forty-five

Scripture: Acts 1:8. "You will be my witnesses in . . . Samaria."

Action: Share some form of Christian witness today with someone who is unlike you culturally, economically, or ethnically.

Prayer: *You are the Lord of all nations. Your name is above every name. Help me live and bear witness beyond my zone of comfort and familiarity.*

Day Forty-six

Scripture: Acts 1:8. "You will be my witnesses . . . to the ends of the earth."

Action: God's love knows no bounds. Pray for experiences of hope and healing in remote communities across the planet.

Prayer: *Thine is the kingdom and the power and the glory.*

Day Forty-seven

Scripture: John 14:18. "I will not leave you orphaned [comfortless]; I am coming to you."

Action: Engage in an act of Christian caregiving today—a visit, a phone call, a prayer, a personal letter.

Prayer: *Help me extend your comfort to someone who is alone today.*

Day Forty-eight

Scripture: Acts 2:1b. "They were all together in one place."

Action: Express your faithfulness to God in the places where God is worshiped and adored.

Prayer: *I am glad to be in your house, O God, offering praise to you.*

Day Forty-nine

A day of rest. Pray for the fruit of the Spirit in your life: "love, joy, peace, patience, kindness, generosity, faithfulness, gentleness, and self-control" (see Galatians 5:22-23a).

Day Fifty—Day of Pentecost

Scripture: Acts 2:17b. "I will pour out my Spirit upon all flesh."

Action: Pray for the church's power among all people, announcing the good news of life and hope.

Prayer: *Send your Spirit upon us, O God, and raise us up to be Easter people, to the glory of your name.*

Have copies of "Fifty Days of Resurrection Living" available in an accessible place adjacent to your worship setting. Permission is granted for use within your church, provided the following credit line is included on each copy: "From *Easter Services, Sermons, and Prayers* by Kenneth H. Carter Jr. Copyright 2007 by Abingdon Press. Reproduced by permission."

Invitation

You might use the following letter to invite participants to experience "Fifty Days of Resurrection Living":

Dear [*Name*],

We will celebrate the resurrection of Jesus this Sunday, [*Date, at Time(s)*]. This is this most significant day of the year for Christians, and we hope you will be present. We also hope you will invite a guest.

We are also asking that you view Easter in a different way this year: not as an ending, but as a beginning. We are offering a simple method for spiritual renewal: *Fifty Days of Resurrection Living.* If you choose to participate, you may pick up a copy of each day's discipline, which is very simple, focused, and yet important in keeping the Easter message of life and hope before you.

May God bless us all in the days ahead, as we are receptive to the good news of Easter!

In Christ,

_____ (pastor)

_____ (*Fifty Days of Resurrection Living* coordinator)

A SERMON SERIES FOR THE EASTER SEASON

Consider offering a series of sermons on Jesus in the weeks following Easter Sunday. Adam Hamilton has often used sermon series as continuations of the highly attended Sundays of the year at the Church of the Resurrection in Kansas City (see his *Unleashing the Word* [Nashville: Abingdon, 2003]). Publicize the series within the congregation and in the local community to help keep energy and attendance high following the Easter celebration (see sample language below). The following series assumes that there is a fascination in both the culture and the church with Jesus.

Easter Sunday—First Sunday: Was Jesus Raised from the Dead?

Scripture:	One of the Gospel narratives about the resurrection (Matthew 28; Mark 16; Luke 24; John 20)
Human Condition:	Absence of hope
Faithful Response:	Live hopefully in this life and the next

Second Sunday: How Can I Believe in Something I Cannot See?

Scripture:	John 20:19-31—The story of Thomas on faith and doubt
Human Condition:	Cynicism and skepticism
Faithful Response:	Live by faith, even in the midst of doubt

Third Sunday: Where Is Jesus in the World?

Scripture:	Luke 24:36-48—The road to Emmaus; why Jesus seems to be hidden at times
Human Condition:	Despair, lack of visible results
Faithful Response:	Stay on the journey with Jesus and his followers

Fourth Sunday: Does Jesus Care About Me?

Scripture:	John 10:11-18—I am the good shepherd; compassion, care for the lost

91

| Human Condition: | Lack of compassion and care for others |
| Faithful Response: | Reach out to those in need of love and friendship |

Fifth Sunday: What Does Jesus Want Me to Be When I Grow Up?

Scripture:	John 15:1-8—Bearing fruit; being a disciple; abiding in Jesus
Human Condition:	Lack of growth, complacency
Faithful Response:	Bear fruit, exercise spiritual disciplines

Sixth Sunday: Does Following Jesus Mean Loving My Neighbor? My Enemy?

Scripture:	John 15:9-17; Matthew 5:43-48— Nature of love
Human Condition:	Difficult or estranged relationships
Faithful Response:	Love others as Jesus loves them

Seventh Sunday: Where Will I End Up if I Follow Jesus?

Scripture:	John 17:9-19—As you sent me into the world, I am sending them
Human Condition:	Drawing inward, isolation from others
Faithful Response:	Share the good news

Eighth Sunday—Pentecost Sunday: Is Jesus Still Alive?

Scripture:	John 14; Acts 2—The Holy Spirit as the ongoing presence of Jesus
Human Condition:	Religion as works righteousness, living out of a duty-orientation
Faithful Response:	Rely on the Spirit/Breath/Wind of God's presence in Jesus Christ

Invitation

The following news release might be sent to a local newspaper or radio station:

> The Rev. *[Name]*, pastor of *[Church Name]*, will be preaching a series of messages on the most important questions of all for Christians: Who is Jesus Christ? What does Jesus mean to us? What is the significance of Jesus for our world today? These messages will begin on Easter Sunday, and all are invited. Contact *[Name]* at *[Phone]* for more information.

The following note might be placed in the Easter Sunday worship bulletin:

> Today's message, *[Sermon Title]*, is the first in a series of sermons on some of the most important questions of all for Christians:
>
> > Who is Jesus Christ?
> > What does Jesus mean to us?
> > What is the significance of Jesus for our world today?
>
> These questions will be explored in messages offered during the next several Sundays. We encourage you to join us and learn more about Jesus in the coming weeks. Why not make the decision this morning to be present for each of these messages, and discover the uniqueness and power of Jesus Christ as you listen, think, pray, and reflect.

RESOURCES

I have found the resources listed below to be helpful in engaging my own imagination in communicating the Easter faith. This is certainly not an exhaustive listing of sources, and you are invited to undertake your own search. In the midst of the current explosion of information that surrounds us, you will find some books out of print, some material available online, and some in varying formats. My advice: seek and you will find!

Brand, Paul, and Philip Yancey. "The Scars of Easter," *Christianity Today Classic.* http://www.christianitytoday.com/ct/2000/116/21.0.html (accessed September 4, 2006).

Callahan, Kennon. *The Future That Has Come* (San Francisco: Jossey-Bass, 2002): Callahan is a church consultant whose work is grounded in a theology of hope for the church's mission in the world. He draws heavily upon themes of resurrection in all of his writings. I am grateful to him personally for learnings related to how a church lives in the resurrection reality.

Handel, George Frideric. *Messiah: A Sacred Oratorio.* Composed 1742: Includes the "Hallelujah Chorus," one of the best-known and most widely loved pieces in all of sacred music. See the helpful website, http://gfhandel.org/messiah.htm, for background information, the libretto, and a list of recommended readings and recordings.

Hays, Richard B. *First Corinthians (Interpretation: A Bible Commentary for Preaching and Teaching)* (Louisville: Westminster John Knox, 1997): This is an invaluable commentary for the preacher who wants to investigate the intricacies of 1 Corinthians 15, our most sustained text related to the resurrection of the body. It is an excellent interpretation of a complex and yet critical facet of the faith.

Johnson, Luke Timothy. *Living Jesus: Learning the Heart of the Gospel* (San Francisco: HarperSanFrancisco, 2000): A concise and accessible introduction to the concept that Jesus is a living reality and not merely a historical memory. Johnson frames the questions in ways that guide the reader to examine his or her own preconceptions about Jesus.

Knowles Wallace, Robin. *Palm Sunday and Holy Week Services (Just in Time!)* (Nashville: Abingdon Press, 2006): A companion to this book that focuses on worship planning and services in the critical days leading up to Easter.

Lawton, Kim. "Easter Hope in Time of War." Interview with Frederick Buechner. *Religion and Ethics Newsweekly*, April 18, 2003. http://www.pbs.org/wnet/religionandethics/week633/feature.html (accessed September 4, 2006): One of our wisest voices in North American Christianity reflects on hope in a hopeless time.

McGrath, Alister. *What Was God Doing on the Cross?* (Eugene, Oreg.: Wipf & Stock Publishers, 1999).

Matthewes-Green, Frederica. "Easter Changes Everything." *Beliefnet.* http://www.beliefnet.com/story/74/story_7448_1.html (accessed September 4, 2006): A creatively odd and yet substantive take on the Easter observance in our culture, from an Orthodox perspective.

Meeks, Blair Gilmer. *Season of Ash and Fire: Prayers and Liturgies for Lent and Easter* (Nashville: Abingdon, 2004): Creative resources in the days prior to and following Easter.

Revised Common Lectionary. http://www.gbod.org/worship/lectionary/default.asp. For those who follow the scheduled biblical texts for worship.

Rutter, John. *Requiem*, composed 1985 (London: Oxford University Press): Includes the refrain "I am the Resurrection and the Life," based upon Jesus' announcement at the tomb of Lazarus (John 10).

Topliffe, Keith Beasley. *Surrendering to God* (Brewster, Mass: Paraclete, 2001).

The United Methodist Book of Worship, edited by Andy Langford (Nashville: The United Methodist Publishing House, 1992). This resource is particularly helpful in setting Easter within the context of its Jewish roots and in explaining the spiritual preparations undertaken in Lent and observed in Holy Week that find their fulfillment on Easter Sunday.

Willow Dramas, Willow Creek Association, South Barrington, Illinois. http://www.willowcreek.com/willowdrama/. These dramas are representative samples of how church drama can be implemented with humor, excellence, and meaning. Most church dramas are too heavy in tone and obvious in the unfolding message. The best of these have a lighter touch, and display a creativity that is welcome if this art form is to have a place, as it should, in the worship of God.

Witherington, Ben. "Rising to the Occasion: Easter Reflections." http://benwitherington.blogspot.com/2006/04/rising-to-occasion-easter-reflections.html (accessed September 4, 2006).

Scripture Index

Judges' Rules. (In Miss Pringle's romances there was commonly a point at which some shady character was told by Catfish that anything he said would be taken down and might be used in evidence: an incident which her more experienced readers knew to be virtually a verdict of Not Guilty delivered on the spot.) But, on the whole, Miss Pringle was satisfied by her performance. Her only regret was that she had not thought up some stratagem for introducing into Lady Pinkerton's drawing-room (at this crucial stage of the affair) the Crime Reporter of *The Times*. But did *The Times* (the London *Times*) *have* a Crime Reporter? Possibly not. In general terms, however, the idea would have been a good one. It was now close on midnight. But, had there been a journalist on hand, it might just have been possible to make one of the later editions of a national daily before it went to bed. In her mind's eye Miss Pringle was seeing, if vaguely, a banner headline, when she was called to present reality by the voice – still the respectful voice, addressed as to his betters – of Detective-Inspector Graves. It was a voice, however, that held a not altogether agreeable property. Almost, indeed, it appeared to speak of worms and epitaphs.

'Thank you very much, madam. What you have to tell me is very interesting. Striking, in a manner of speaking. Decidedly striking. And we seem to have a little time in hand. If, that's to say, your calculations are correct, and this gentleman we've been hearing about wholly reliable.' Graves consulted his watch. 'Just under fifteen minutes. And as Sir Ambrose is with us in this room, his bacon – if I may express it in that vulgar way, madam – appears safe enough.'

'And how thankful I am!' Miss Pringle said. She remembered to clasp her hands in a kind of secular ecstasy. 'But we must remember that the incendiary device – '

'Quite so, madam. But let me remind you that, as a result of your very public-spirited telephone message, I have a number of officers posted round the house. And even one up beside the stable clock itself. You are quite sure that the detonator is sited there?'

'Perfectly.' Miss Pringle was entirely firm. 'And contrived so as to be activated by a twelfth stroke only.'

'Commendably ingenious,' Appleby said. It was the first comment he had offered.

'Thank you,' Miss Pringle responded, much gratified. Then,

bethinking herself, she added, 'How little I imagined that so harmless a stroke of fiction should be put to – '

'Quite so,' Appleby said. 'Absolutely quite so. But my colleague must forgive me for interrupting him.' At this point Appleby accepted a cigar from Sir Ambrose, to whom an exact hospitality appeared to be the one remaining resource. 'I think he may conceivably have one or two questions to ask. In the interest of subsidiary elucidation, that is to say.' At this Appleby offered Miss Pringle a brief glance – such as perhaps might be due to a performing animal of extraordinary accomplishment in a circus. 'And I won't interrupt again.'

'Thank you,' Graves said – quite with the rapid deftness of one practised participant to another practised participant in a television *causerie*. 'If I may, madam, run over a few salient points?'

'Please do,' Miss Pringle said composedly. 'Deeply culpable as I feel – '

'Quite so. But you have been, if I may say so, extraordinarily acute in tumbling to the abominable deception imposed on you.' Graves, who seemed to learn rapidly, articulated this with a smoothness that would have done credit to the retired Commissioner of Metropolitan Police himself. 'Captain Bulkington, whose acquaintance you had made quite by chance, had expressed himself as attracted by the idea of entering into the field of detective fiction: a kind of writing – of literature, indeed – in which you are recognized as being something more than in the top ten.'

'You are very kind,' Miss Pringle said. It occurred to her that Sir Ambrose Pinkerton, so adequate in finding her a chair, had for some reason neglected to offer her brandy. She was beginning to feel the need of it. What she had imbibed earlier in the Jolly Chairman had now failed of its effect. It had probably been of deplorably inferior quality. 'But go on,' Miss Pringle said. And she added courageously, 'Time presses.'

'*Tempus fugit.*' For the first time, Lady Appleby had looked up from her crochet. 'As Captain Bulkington might say.'

'So you agreed,' Graves pursued, 'to suggest to Captain Bulkington, chiefly through a series of letters, the plot of a story which might suitably be entitled *The Three Warnings*, or something of the sort. All this about Earth, Air, Fire, and Water. Or, to be more precise, Air, Water, Earth, and Fire. And you little knew – I think that would be your way of expressing the matter – that Captain Bulkington was proposing, in sober actuality – '

'Just so,' Miss Pringle said heroically. 'On the first day, or night, of the fourth month. In fact, *now*.'

'Have you any idea why Captain Bulkington should propose to release these shocking engines upon Sir Ambrose and his household?'

Appleby, who had been sitting with his right leg crossed negligently over his left, stirred slightly and crossed his left leg over his right. It might have been his manner of acknowledging that the note-taking Detective-Inspector Graves possessed unsuspected, because cunningly dissimulated, rhetorical resources.

'Really none whatever,' Miss Pringle said firmly. 'The man must be mad.'

'You are not alone in suggesting that point of view. But now, another point. I am not quite clear as to how sudden illumination – if I may put it that way – came to you, madam. The horrid truth, as it were. The occasion or prompting of your picking up a telephone and communicating with the police.'

'Intuition, Inspector.' What was surely Miss Pringle's supreme moment had come. 'Something stirred in the deep well.'

'The deep *well*?' For the first time in this curious encounter, Detective-Inspector Graves appeared really startled.

'The deep well of unconscious cerebration.'

This – reasonably enough – produced silence. It was a silence broken, first, by a faint whirr: nothing less than the premonitory signal which large clocks are in the habit of offering five minutes before gathering up their forces to strike the hour. And then, more decisively, it was broken by Miss Anketel.

'Good God!' Miss Anketel said. 'What balderdash is all this? Sir John, will you be so good as to assist us to a little common sense?'

But it didn't look as if Appleby was disposed to oblige. His cigar was burning evenly, and he appeared entirely relaxed.

'As I keep on saying,' he presently and mildly remarked, 'we simply wait and see. Four minutes and thirty seconds, or thereabout.'

This small interval of time elapsed. The peaceful silence which

141

darkest Wiltshire enjoys in the dead waste and middle of the night remained unbroken. No owl hooted or pheasant clacked. From the populous stables of the Pinkertons not a neigh or whinny was heard. And Miss Pringle paled, as one who is betrayed. Observing this, Sir Ambrose was tardily recalled to the duties of his station. He rose and advanced upon this incredible woman, bottle in hand.

'A drop of this?' Sir Ambrose sympathetically asked.

'Thank you.' Faintly, Miss Pringle nodded. And then she spoke out, loud and clear. 'The scoundrel must have lost his nerve,' she declared.

'Which isn't true of you,' Appleby said. He spoke with honest admiration – but spoke too soon. For Miss Priscilla Pringle (talented authoress of *Poison at the Parsonage*) had risen and bolted from the room.

Chapter Twenty

John Appleby followed. He did so with a gesture indicating his persuasion that an effect of general hue and cry was not desirable. Judith would not in any case have abandoned her crochet; the day had passed when she judged it amusing to join her husband in policemanly scampers. The Pinkertons and Miss Anketel merely exchanged glances of politely restrained relief, thereby registering their sense that Miss Pringle had proved not at all their sort of person. Detective-Inspector Graves, having acquitted himself with credit, was perfectly willing to take Appleby's raised finger as a command, and he gave himself placidly to tidying up his notes. The result of all this was that Appleby presently found himself on the terrace of Long Canings Hall, alone under the stars – except for the presence of a few looming forms which might have been either heathen divinities or Wiltshire constables.

The police were certainly not evident in any active role. Assembled and stationed for the purpose of intervening to prevent the spectacular destruction of a substantial manor house and its owner, they had not been required to interfere with the departure of a solitary female guest. And that Miss Pringle had indeed departed was evident from the sound of a motor-engine retreating down the drive – from this and the sudden appearance of wavering headlights as the lady remembered to switch them on.

But now a car was advancing from the other direction, and in a moment it could be seen that the two were passing each other. Then, rather dashingly, the on-coming vehicle circled the broad gravel sweep before the house, and came to a halt more or less under Appleby's nose. It was the sort of car in which most of the available space is given over to the works, and the occupants edge themselves in as they may. But the driver who scrambled from the sporting conveyance was the Reverend Dr Howard.

'Ah, Sir John again!' Howard said. 'And I think that was our friend Miss Pringle who has just driven away.'

'You recognized her?'

'I recognized her car. I once changed a wheel on it when she had a puncture in Gibber. So far as I am concerned, her presence adds to the mystery by which we appear to be surrounded. Are those people in the manor all right? And the good Miss Anketel? It's really what I came to find out.'

'They are all in excellent health, I'm glad to say. So you have felt able to leave your young fugitive?'

'Jenkins? My housekeeper will hold his hand if he wakes up sobbing in the night. He has been talking the most extraordinary stuff.'

'Has he, indeed? If you don't feel it to be too chilly, Howard, let us take a turn round the house. A little conversation may be useful.'

'By all means. But you have no sense of a crisis that won't keep?'

'Not on my present information. There is a certain intrepidity about Miss Pringle, although I think she is prone to exist in considerable confusion of mind. Just at the moment, I expect that she is on the way to "Kandahar". It doesn't seem a move that can much mend matters, from her rather peculiar point of view. Whether she is placing herself at some sort of hazard, or is on the contrary disposed so to place the learned Bulkington, is another matter. I hope, as a matter of fact, that you can help me to a clearer view of it.'

Dr Howard received this for a moment in silence, and the two men together rounded a corner of the building. A sickle moon here shed upon spreading lawns a dubious radiance that died before the low dark mass of surrounding shrubberies. In the middle of this composition, like a great rock rearing itself out of a still sea, stood a single cedar. Howard paused to view it thoughtfully.

'Am I right,' he asked, 'in thinking that that tree was mixed up with one of the tomfooleries which have been worrying Pinkerton?'

'Certainly. Pinkerton found a hanged Pinkerton in it. And he found a drowned Pinkerton and a buried Pinkerton as well.'

'Did he, indeed?' Impatience before folly was perceptible in Dr Howard's tone. 'Am I right in thinking that whatever precisely has been happening has been a very great deal of nonsense – somehow involving both Bulkington and that inquisitive Miss Pringle, but so silly as scarcely to be worth elucidation?'

'I'm afraid I don't really know.' Appleby glanced whimsically at the rector in the moonlight. 'I shan't know until I *have* elucidated it. Fortunately, the greater part of the job is already done. The follies of Miss Pringle – and I think they are fairly to be called follies rather than crimes – are no longer obscure to me. With your neighbour Captain Bulkington it is another matter. I confess to being a little uneasy about him. He has a great appearance of absurdity of a not unendearing sort. One feels, so to speak, like letting him off with a caution. And yet I wonder. I wonder – and should be most interested to know how this strikes you – whether he may not be a rather notably wicked person.'

'Ah!'

'Precisely, Howard! "Ah" is the word. Take, for instance, those two youths, Waterbird and Jenkins. It would be quite unfair, I believe, to claim there is any evidence that Bulkington has in a serious sense corrupted them. He appears, indeed, to have introduced them to the possibilities of fornication –'

'Good God, sir! Don't you call that corruption?'

'Well, yes – I do. But I wouldn't say there was anything positively heinous about it. Incidentally, it was a means of establishing a hold over them, which he has exploited in order to compel them to carry out a number of pranks which they must have judged senseless and more or less harmless. Pranks reflecting, as it happens, the fanciful mind of our friend Miss Pringle. But dismiss that for a moment. I am not sure that I don't find something more disturbing – something hinting Bulkington to be more wicked than absurd – in whatever it is that has really got young Ralph Jenkins down. According to Miss Anketel – and this is something you encountered along with her, and must be in a position to confirm – Bulkington has been drinking heavily and behaving in an alarmingly manic fashion. And Jenkins has been particularly scared by something that has to do with that abandoned well in the Old Rectory garden.'

'Ah, the well! So we come back to that.'

'Indeed, we do,' Appleby said. 'And to the death of Dr Pusey.'

They had reached an end of the terrace which terminated in a squat balustrade. On this Dr Howard now casually perched himself – much as he had done on the dangerously low coping of the fatal well itself. He then waited for Appleby to do the same. His ease of manner, however, was not immediately reflected in his speech.

'How sorry I am,' he said, 'that I cannot help you more with a piece of ancient history which appears so much to interest you. But it was before my time, as I have said.'

'No doubt. But at least the present perturbation of Ralph Jenkins, and his affecting flight, my dear rector, to the sanctuary of Holy Church, is well within your cognizance. And it's that I'd be grateful if I might hear a little more about. It might help me when I go over to "Kandahar".'

'You're going over there at this hour?' Howard asked. He seemed startled. 'The business requires following up at that pace?'

'It may. I don't know. One has to be on the safe side, does one not? And now, please, the mind of Ralph Jenkins.'

'Very well. What the wretched boy says is roughly this. Waterbird has lately been making him spy closely on Bulkington. Waterbird plans for Bulkington some hideous reversal of fortune. His favourite phrase, it seems, is that he is going to have the Bulgar howling yet. They are really an awful set.'

'No doubt. But then?'

'Jenkins, compelled to espionage at the expense of his own innocent slumbers, has discovered that Bulkington gets up and prowls in the small hours. He goes outside and wanders around – in narrowing circles which gradually bring him closer and closer to that damned well. Eventually he reaches it, and when he reaches it he gloats.'

'Gloats? That would be Jenkins's word?'

'Precisely. He gloats. And, having gloated, he delivers himself of peal upon peal of maniacal laughter.'

'*Not* Jenkins's word?'

'Not exactly – but that is the idea. And then Bulkington goes back to bed. That is Jenkins's entire story. Perhaps, Appleby, you make more of it than I do.'

'I think not,' Appleby said. 'I think you find it highly suggestive.'

'I fail to understand you.'

'Again, I think not. The wretched Jenkins's narrative has re-kindled in your mind suspicions which you have been glad to forget, or to half-forget, concerning the death of your predecessor. We have really – you and I – had this out on the carpet before. But we didn't then go through with it. Let us do so now.'

'Very well.'

'Your mind revolts violently – and I sympathize with you – at the thoughts of scandal attaching to a fellow Clerk in Holy Orders. Better that some wicked man go free than that such an evil, deeply injurious to the faith of your flock, should befall. Am I right?'

'I have to say Yes. Matters would scarcely be improved' – Howard could be seen to smile grimly in the faint moonlight – 'by my starting in on a pack of lies.'

'I'd expect nothing of the kind. So where are we? We have to suppose that Pusey, poor man, had succumbed to some snare of the devil which the world (although pretty well the devil's property) would judge very bad indeed. We can imagine this or that – from melting down the church plate to the most striking sins of the flesh. His usher, this wretched cashiered or half-pay Bulk-ington, finds him out, and bleeds him white. That's where the money came from for buying up what was then quite a flourishing tutorial establishment when the moment arrived. And it arrived, of course, when Pusey was drowned. But how did he come to drown? There arrived a stage at which he felt, as so many victims of ruthless blackmail have come to feel, that his situation was insupportable, and that he must find his own way out. But he had the credit of the cloth to consider. He was Pusey, D.D. – *sanctae theologiae professor*. *S.T.P.* for short. Am I right?'

'It is my conjecture.'

'He formed a habit of sitting on the well, reading his novel, his breviary, or whatever. He feigned the progressive development of some bodily infirmity characterized by dizzy fits. Having thus done his duty, he drowned himself. *In a well*, Howard! Think of it.'

'I often have.'

'And you have felt that, not merely as a priest but also as a man, his name was to be protected, even if it meant that Bulkington –'

'You need not dot the *i*'s and cross the *t*'s.'

'I beg your pardon. But well – ' Appleby broke off. 'One hesitates to use the word, even as a different part of speech. But, well, that is it.'

'Yes.' Dr Howard sighed softly. 'Do you know? I'm glad, now, that we've got so far.'

'It is a clarification.' Appleby spoke dispassionately. 'Conjectural, perhaps, but we both accept it. So what is the result?'

'It is for you to say.'

'Our bizarre comedy – Miss Pringle's nonsense, Bulkington's present mere or near nonsense – becomes *comédie noire*. Half a mile away from us at this moment there is a thoroughly evil man.' Appleby paused. 'So again, what follows?'

'Those young men must be got clear of him, for a start. I ought to have seen that long ago.'

'I am bound to say I think you should. However, Jenkins, at least, is in sanctuary.'

'Don't mock me, Appleby.'

'My dear man, heaven forbid.' Again Appleby paused. 'And now I am going to walk over and have a word with him.'

'And with Miss Pringle?'

'If she is there, yes. She, too, must be got away, if it can be done.'

Chapter Twenty-one

That considerable confusion of mind which Appleby had predicated of Miss Pringle could not have been said to be abating in her as she drove through the darkness on her way to 'Kandahar'. Captain Bulkington, she chiefly felt, had let her down badly. His nerve must have failed him in a craven manner particularly reprehensible and contemptible in one bred to the profession of arms. As a result, she had performed much labour, and suffered much anxiety, wholly in vain. There was going to be no sensation at all – except, perhaps of a very minor sort calculated to do nothing but bring a certain amount of unkindly ridicule upon herself. Barbara Vanderpump would certainly tell their common friends that dear Priscilla had been most oddly imagining things. The odious man Appleby might make a kind of smoking-room story out of the affair, and retail it to his cronies at his club. But of anything worthy to be called publicity there would be nothing at all. That treacherous policeman Graves, with his disgusting servility towards the local grandees, would simply accept instructions to drop the whole thing. The official line would be that Bulkington had gone so far as to arrange for the commission of a few tasteless practical jokes, but beyond this no evil had been plotted except within the confines of her own imagination. And thus would decorum, repose, and the avoidance of any breath of public scandal be secured in this stupid little part of Wiltshire. The plain fact was that Bulkington had (as she believed her nephew Timothy would express it) made a monkey of her. It was all very mortifying indeed.

These thoughts angered Miss Pringle very much, and it is surely an instance of the largeness of spirit in this noble woman that she saw nothing in them to occasion alarm. Cold prudence would doubtless have suggested that she heed the first sign-post pointing in the direction of Worcestershire; that she should, in fact, cut her losses (which were in the main merely of time and, perhaps, self-conceit), lie low for a month or two, and do her best never to think of Long Canings again. Captain Bulkington had proved in the event, indeed, less lethal than she had hoped, but the record displayed him clearly enough as an eccentric, unreliable, malicious, and perhaps tricky character: somebody to give a wide berth to unless in the interest of some positive benefit to oneself. Such a benefit to Miss Pringle was no longer in question. She was seeking out the Captain now to no better purpose than that of permitting herself the luxury of giving him a piece of her mind. Yes – there can be no doubt whatever that Miss Pringle would have done better to go home.

'My fair temptress, 'pon my soul!' Captain Bulkington said – and produced a high cackle of a laugh which Miss Pringle did not recall quite to have heard before. He had opened his front-door himself. 'Come to lighten my solitude. Capital thing. Come in.'

'Your solitude?' Miss Pringle echoed. Instinctive propriety, as ever, was strong in her. 'But I take it that your housekeeper – ?'

'Sleeps in the village, my dear. And as for those two louts, they're both past history, praise God. Jenkins has absconded, and Waterbird has walked out. There's a difference, you know – what you might call a technical difference. Jenkins slunk off. It upset Waterbird, and he had a word with me. He'd have had *words* with me if I'd given him the chance. As it was, he got in one or two disobliging things. If I'd been thirty years younger, he said, he'd have left me a couple of black eyes to remember him by.' Rather surprisingly, Captain Bulkington chuckled again on a frankly joyous note. 'Good riddance, eh? And leaves you my only resource, my dear. So come into my sanctum. Come into my parlour, said the spider to the fly. Ha, ha!'

It was suddenly borne in upon Miss Pringle that she was now closeted with a near-madman in an empty house in a retired situation. She had rather forgotten the madness of Bulkington. It seemed pretty apparent now. Suddenly, too, there was borne in upon her a realization of the irrationality of her own present position. She had come to denounce Bulkington. But for what? For failing to murder a harmless if tiresome neighbour? Or for failing to allow himself to be detected and apprehended in an attempt at such a murder? The second of these reproaches (if overheard by third parties) would surely sound even dottier than the first. There was, of course, what might be called the formal position: she had provided – all-trustingly – a kind of correspondence course in detective literature, and Bulkington had made perverted use of her ideas by using them to launch at least a minor campaign of terror against Sir Ambrose Pilkington, Bart. But that didn't, somehow, now seem a very promising line. She would really do better simply to hit Bulkington on the head with her umbrella, and go away. Unfortunately she wasn't provided with an umbrella so this course wasn't practicable. So what line was she to take?

The problem proved to be one she didn't have to face, since Captain Bulkington took a brisk initiative himself. He looked Miss Pringle up and down – rather in the manner of a woman expertly deciding where another woman does her shopping, or perhaps of the sort of person who guesses your age or your weight at a fair.

'£5,000,' Captain Bulkington said.

'I beg your pardon?' There was perplexity in Miss Pringle's voice. She didn't take this in at all.

'You can run to it easily.' Captain Bulkington knew what he was talking about. 'Even if it's not in your current account, the bank will make no bones about protecting your interest by honouring the cheque.'

Miss Pringle was about to say, 'I think you must be insane'. But a writer dislikes the enunciation of lame half-truths, and she decided to hold her peace.

'Times change,' Captain Bulkington said comfortably. 'It was a mere £500 we talked about before. And that trifle was to pass in the other direction – ha-ha! *Tempus fugit*, *tempus edax* something-or-other.'

'Do you have the impertinence to suggest that there is some pressing reason why I should pay you a large sum of money?' Miss Pringle spoke boldly, but she was not really feeling very bold. What she *was* feeling might best have been described as the menace of the unknown. Bulkington was extravagantly pleased with himself, and she couldn't at all guess why. Of course the whole situation was extremely awkward and delicate – but then it was surely that for this dreadful man quite as much as for herself. Had he something up his sleeve? She very much feared that this must be the state of the case. 'If there is any question of compensation,' Miss Pringle continued somewhat wildly, 'it ought certainly to be the other way round. For several months now, I have been put to much trouble and expense.'

'Ah! And to what purpose, my dear? Just tell me what you think it had all been in aid of.'

'I undertook to supply you with the materials for a harmless romance. Greatly to my embarrassment, you have used them – or part of them – for the outrageous purpose of harassing an inoffensive gentleman. A landed gentleman' – Miss Pringle amplified with emphasis – 'resident in this county.' For a moment it seemed to her that this was quite a hopeful line to take, after all. 'And I am by no means certain that you might not have gone further still.'

'I'll bet you're not.' Captain Bulkington produced his spine-chilling chuckle. 'Just a few red-faced dummies littering the old idiot's park! There wouldn't be much in *that* for you to base your blackguardly blackmail on.'

'My *what*?'

'It's what you've been after, isn't it? I saw it in your face, the first time we met. I even saw it in the face of Orlando your cat.' Captain Bulkington found this imbecile and offensive pleasantry so amusing that he roared with laughter. 'Well, I thought I'd have you on. Lead you a little up the garden path, my dear. See just how far *you* would go. And I'm full of admiration, mind you. You've been most fiendishly clever.'

Miss Pringle, although remaining sufficiently rational to question the justice of this commendation, could not suppress a small glow of gratification. Still, it was beginning to look as if, to escape from this developing nightmare, she would have to be very clever indeed.

'You've kept your options open,' Captain Bulkington said, 'and that's always a great thing. Your weakness, if I may say so, has been on the psychological side. I'm a very simple fellow, you know, and at the same time what you might call the very type of the rational man.' As the Captain thus characterized himself he looked – it seemed to Miss Pringle – rather more indisputably mad than he had ever done before. 'You thought of me as an unbalanced sort of chap, who had developed a senseless hatred of that idiot Pinkerton, and who might be coaxed into the commission of nothing less than *un crime gratuit*.'

'I don't know what you mean.' Miss Pringle recognized the feebleness of her remark even as she uttered it. She did, of course, know perfectly well what is meant by this French expression, nor ought she to have been surprised that Captain Bulkington (engaged, as he was, in the higher education of the young) commanded it. She *was* surprised, all the same. And she was becoming thoroughly unnerved as well.

'Your idea was that, if you played your cards cleverly, there would be either the most splendid publicity in the affair or a good round sum in your pocket to induce you to keep me out of the picture. That's what I mean by keeping your options open.'

'I never for a moment – ' Miss Pringle fell silent, baffled. She had never, of course, considered the remote possibility of extracting money from Bulkington. It was only too clear, for one thing, that

151

he hadn't any. But it seemed that her actual intention had been lucid to him almost from the first. And this humiliated Miss Pringle. It was like having a reader tumble to the solution of one of her baffling mysteries not much further on that Chapter Four or Five.

'What you failed to consider,' Captain Bulkington went on, 'was that the endeavour to coax me into crime might well be criminal in itself.'

'The endeavour to coax you – ?' It came to Miss Pringle that she had, in fact, done something very like this. Fortunately, it had been on an occasion strictly *tête-à-tête*. 'You are talking utter nonsense,' she said coldly.

'Then let us hear a little of the evidence, my dear.' As he spoke, Captain Bulkington moved across his sanctum and made some small movement of a hand which, for the moment, Miss Pringle was unable to interpret. And, immediately, a third voice was heard in the room. But it wasn't, strictly, a *third* voice. It was Miss Pringle's own voice – unrecognizable except by an effort, as one's own recorded voice commonly is.

'*Kidnapping?*' Miss Pringle heard herself say – unmistakably on a note of disappointment.

'*Kidnapping? I'm afraid that kidnapping wouldn't interest me very much. I'd scarcely consider myself competent to work out anything of the kind, or to give you an effective hand at it. Murder is another matter. I could put you on the rails there.*'

'*Ha, ha! We understand each other, wouldn't you say?*'

'*I am sure we do. Sir Ambrose is to be your victim. He is going to be killed, and the killer is going to get away with it. But just who – I mean, what sort of person – is going to commit the crime? Have you at all thought, for instance, of somebody rather like yourself?*'

'*Ha, ha, ha! Kidnapping and murder! How about that?*'

'*Arson could be got in, too.*'

'*Arson's quite an idea. Yes, arson attracts me.*'

'*Captain Bulkington, have you considered what means we might take to launch this joint enterprise?*'

'*Suggest you move in here.*'

'*It would be best to proceed differently. I suggest that we correspond, but there is one condition which must be observed. We have been led into talking at times almost as if we were contemplating real crime – '*

'Good Lord! But you're entirely right. Extraordinary thing.'

'A mere shorthand, of course.'

'Just that. You express it deuced well.'

'A façon de parler, *in fact.'*

'Quite so, quite so.'

'My own letters will be strictly about the writing of a book. Your own will observe a similar discretion.'

'Damned good tip. About the money now. Remember some mention of £500? Would that be about right, if we brought the thing off?'

'For the mere technical know-how for a single simple murder it would be a most adequate remuneration.'

Thus confusedly did there come to Miss Pringle an ingeniously cut version of what had been a rambling and predominantly scatty conversation. Such was her perturbation, she was hearing it only imperfectly, perhaps, in its edited form. But two impressions remained with her. It had been reduced to something more or less businesslike in tone. And her own voice, intermittently at least, was heavy with a coarse conspiratorial irony!

'Interesting, eh?' the Captain was saying. 'Two ways of taking it, of course. Either, my dear, you were selling murder and are of interest to the police as a consequence, or you had some crackpot notion in your head that would make you the laughing stock of England. So – as I said – £5,000.'

Chapter Twenty-two

The situation was one which a lower-class criminal (uncommon in Miss Pringle's fictions) might have pronounced a fair cop. Miss Pringle was amazed that the extreme vulnerability of her grand design had not been evident to her from the first. The least disastrous issue of it now appeared to be that she would presently figure in the public prints as a harmless crackpot. 'Crackpot' had been Captain Bulkington's word, and it was rankling. It was doing this because, through all her confusion and dismay, Miss Pringle quite clearly perceived that it was the Captain who was *really* mad. Cunning, yes – but also deeply mad as well. Sooner or later, they would have to lock him up. And they wouldn't have to lock *her* up – or not, at least, in any institution for the mentally deranged. To think of Captain Bulkington ending his days in such a place (perhaps years after having had £5,000 out of her) was really rather sad. Was it not – come to think of it – unbearable? At this point Miss Pringle recalled that she had an emergency plan.

'Very well,' Miss Pringle said composedly. 'We must talk. But not in this room. It has been bugged once, and may be bugged again.' She paused on this, pleased that, even in crisis, the technical terminology of her craft did not desert her. 'And not in this house, either. We'll settle things up, if you please, in the open air.'

'After one a.m.?' Captain Bulkington said dubiously. 'Mild weather, of course. Still, perhaps a bit chilly for a lady – eh?' He paused on this really rather touching solicitude. 'And particularly for a lady of uncertain years.' Achieving this gratuitous piece of malice at the expense of his intended victim of hideous blackmail, Captain Bulkington laughed loudly. He laughed again – and this time his laugh turned into the maniacal cackle. Miss Pringle, if intimidated, was encouraged as well.

They went into the hall of 'Kandahar', and Captain Bulkington opened the front door. The hall was an ill-lit and gloomy place, and Miss Pringle might well have missed the fact that the Captain had unobtrusively possessed himself of a stout walking-stick. She marked this, however, and immediately rather wished she had something of the sort herself. But within reach there was nothing more suitable for assisting a pedestrian than a medium-sized ebony elephant – trumpeting with up-raised trunk – which stood on a table near the door. Captain Bulkington was now for a moment preoccupied with reaching for a deer-stalker hat from a peg. Miss Pringle grabbed the elephant – conveniently by his trunk – and thrust it beneath what was fortunately a voluminous coat. It was a stage in the emergency plan.

Night, silence, and the untended gardens of 'Kandahar' received the late collaborators in a labour of detective literature.

'It is useless,' Miss Pringle said firmly, 'to be unrealistic. For *either* of us to be unrealistic. Compromise must be achieved.'

'Compromise fiddlesticks!' Captain Bulkington barked into the darkness. Argument had been going on for some minutes, during which the two contracting parties had rounded the house and entered what Miss Pringle uncertainly sensed as an abandoned kitchen garden. A moon of sorts had appeared – punctually, she supposed – on the eastern horizon, and she could now sufficiently distinguish the Captain's form beside her to bash him tolerably accurately on the head. But just where was the well? On the last occasion of her leaving 'Kandahar' (and before making her way to the Jolly Chairman and the unexpected society of Messrs Waterbird and Jenkins) she had taken care to make a rapid survey of Captain Bulkington's policies. She could not confidently feel, however, that in the near-darkness her bearings were going to be at all easy to find.

And, meantime, she played for time. She talked in a prolix and confusing way about her finances. She protested her inability to find anything like £5,000 – but she was careful to do this on a note of progressively weakening resolve. As a result, she hoped, Captain Bulkington was feeling he could afford to humour her – as he had done, it might be said, in agreeing to these negotiations taking place thus eccentrically *en plein air*.

But – once more – *where was the well?* It was essential to her emergency plan that she should be able to tumble the corpse into it. If a man falls down a very deep well there is nothing more likely than that he should knock his brains out in the process. Miss Pringle's professional studies had made her quite clear on this point. Whereas if the same man is found merely sprawled in his kitchen garden –

At this point Miss Pringle's meditations were interrupted by a scream. She had – she realized, much to her surprise – uttered it herself. And she had done this because she had seen a ghost.

At least she had seen a white and hovering presence of uncertain dimensions not much more than a dozen yards away. It might have been a sheeted dwarf. It might have been an ectoplasmic apparition in a state of semi-deliquescence. In fact, it was the 'Kandahar' goat. And – quite suddenly – it was no longer hovering. It was hurling itself in Miss Pringle's direction with almost incredible velocity.

Well was it for Miss Pringle in that moment that she was under the protection of a military man. The goat had ingeniously swerved in its charge, very much as if indelicately proposing that its impact upon Miss Pringle should be of posterior effect. But Captain Bulkington (who had produced a roar of manly rage) took two steps forward and lashed out at the creature with his stick. And at this the creature gave a yelp of agony (it was almost a human sound, and Miss Pringle, for some reason, didn't like it at all) before turning and vanishing into the night.

And now Miss Pringle and Captain Bulkington resumed their deliberations and their stroll. Not that it was exactly a stroll. For the Captain's pace was quickening, and there was something obscurely purposive about the course he steered. Miss Pringle had a sense of it as a circular or spiral course, narrowing towards a point. Had she been in a condition of mind apt for recalling the English poets, she might have felt herself in the condition of a pern in a gyre.

And Captain Bulkington was only half-attending to her. She was sure he was determined to have his £5,000. But now there was something else on his mind. He was muttering to himself as he moved. Once or twice he stopped, and produced his weird and gloating cackle of laughter. Then he would press on again, warily but urgently, towards an unseen goal.

Then, suddenly, the well was in front of them.

So was the goat. It seemed to have established itself as what might be called (again in a poetic context) the Guardian of the Well. Captain Bulkington appeared particularly to resent this. He hurled at the goat certain words quite unfit to be heard by ladies. The goat (although itself probably a gentleman) seemed to find them equally distasteful, for it drew away until no more than a white blur again.

Miss Pringle saw that her moment had come. Captain Bulkington still didn't trust the goat; he had half turned and was confronting its dim form with up-raised stick. It was now or never, Miss Pringle told herself, for bringing another animal on the scene. She unbuttoned her coat with her left hand, and thus gained egress for the elephant which was clutched by the trunk in her right. Taking a stealthy step backwards the better to calculate her aim, she raised the elephant high in the air.

It wasn't – alas! – any good. It was no good at all. In the golden world of Miss Pringle's fiction the thing would have been accomplished in a moment. But this was the brazen world of fact. In it – Miss Pringle blindingly and despairingly discovered – she hadn't a scrap of criminal ruthlessness to her name. She could no more bash the unspeakable Bulkington on the head than she could similarly have bashed her dear father the Archdeacon. It was simply not on.

Miss Pringle cried her horror aloud, so that Captain Bulkington turned back and stared at her. The heavy black object she held in her hand was now shameful and intolerable to her, so that she violently cast it away. In this the strength of frenzy must have come to her – for the elephant, although merely lobbed as a schoolgirl might lob a cricket-ball, soared in a bold parabola, was for a moment lost against the darkness of the sky, and then fell (as if most infallibly aimed) plumb into the centre of the well. And it must even have found a gap in the miserable piece of wire-netting covering the thing. It had vanished without a trace.

'What was that?' It was now the turn of Captain Bulkington to cry out with extreme violence, much as if some shrine had been profaned. The well, after all (although Miss Pringle was unaware of the fact), was sacred to him as the scene or instrument of what he may reasonably have regarded as the height of his professional achievement: the hounding to his death of the miserable Dr Pusey many years before. Captain Bulkington ran forward with a further shout of senseless rage, leant over the low, crumbling wall, and peered into the blackness below.

It was the goat's moment. Still doubtless smarting from the thwacking it had received, the creature put down its head and charged. There was a crumbling of masonry, a splintering of rotten wood, a single ghastly shriek, and Captain A. G. de P. Bulkington (of 'Kandahar' and the Imperial Forces Club) had gone ruining after his ebony elephant to the depths below. As for the goat, it gave Miss Pringle a single contemptuous look, and withdrew quietly from the scene. It had shown her, one might say, how such a job ought to be done.

And thus, ten minutes later, Appleby found the lady. She was weeping, she was wildly distraught, but she did manage to tell the tale of the last agony of Captain Bulkington. Appleby found himself not doubting it for a moment – if only because no self-respecting novelist (such as Miss Pringle was) would venture to invent such a catastrophe. His pocket-torch, indeed, did reveal the tracks of the Captain's four-footed executioner. But it would have taken a searchlight to penetrate to the bottom of the well, and it was obvious that there was nothing whatever to be done. It would be a job for the local fire brigade to restore the mortal remains of Bulkington to upper air.

'What shall I do?' Miss Pringle wailed. 'Oh, whatever shall I do?'

It wasn't an easy question to deal with. Appleby, after all, was a policeman. Yet it was hard, somehow, to regard the stricken authoress of *Vengeance at the Vicarage* and other romances except in a sympathetic light. So Appleby countered with a question of his own.

'Miss Pringle, does anybody know you came on here from the Pinkertons?'

'Oh, no – no, Sir John. Nobody at all! The housekeeper sleeps in the village. And those horrible young men have both run away.'

'And your car's in the drive?'

'Yes, indeed. It is just short of the front door.'

Appleby's answer had come to him.

'Get into it quick,' he said, 'and go home.'